Acknowledgment

We will forever be thankful to our dear friend and former pastor, Charles Tope, who came to our home in 1975 to ask us if we would begin making disciples at our church like we had been doing in our home for the past five years. Brother Tope encouraged us to make *One on One with God* available to everyone, not just a few.

Now, twenty-seven years later, thousands of people have been discipled through *One on One with God,* in four languages and in several countries. We thank Brother Tope for allowing God to use him to challenge us and stretch our vision to include reaching the world for Christ through *One on One with God.*

And a special thank you to our dear friends, former pastor, Dr. Anthony Jordan, and our current pastor, Dr. Craig Etheredge, for their continuing encouragement and strong support for *One on One with God.*

Forewords

Max D. Barnett:

The focus on knowing Christ in a progressive, intimate way and then making Him known to others isn't a program to go through, but a lifestyle to develop. Knowing Christ intimately, then giving your life to developing others into disciple–makers is the goal—so that people everywhere can come to know our magnificent Lord, Jesus Christ.

I know of no greater need in the church today than to help its members have an intimate relationship with Christ and then be able to disciple others.

To fulfill this need is what *One on One with God* is all about. The original intent of Jerry and Marilyn Fine was not to develop a discipleship program for others to use. They personally gave their lives to discipling people and as they did, *One on One with God* was born.

In their local church and as Jerry traveled in his career, they discipled people using the materials they developed. Thus, *One on One with God* came into existence over a period of many years in the context of real life situations.

It worked well with an individual or a small group, and with people of various ages. Many becoming Christ's disciples wanted to disciple others. Eventually a leader's guide was developed so anyone could use the materials.

Working with university students, I have seen God use this material to give students direction, a plan, content and confidence that enables them to produce multiplying disciples.

Now there are people scattered around the world using these materials as a guide. Spiritual multiplication is the result.

I hope you will find *One on One with God* as helpful as have thousands of others in knowing Christ personally and developing Christians into disciple–makers.

Max D. Barnett
University of Oklahoma
Baptist Collegiate Ministry

Dr. Anthony L. Jordan:

I had the privilege of serving as pastor of the Northwest Baptist Church, Oklahoma City, for nearly fifteen years. In the early months of my pastorate I discerned a remarkable level of spiritual maturity among the members of the church. It was evident in their commitment to service, prayer life and walk with God. It was apparent to me that the devotional life of the congregation was on a higher plane than most churches. It took only a short time for me to find the source of this maturity.

Northwest had been blessed with godly pastors who preached the Word, and that certainly contributed to the growth of the people. However, I am convinced the greater reason was that hundreds of members had been discipled in a study called *One on One with God.*

This study, developed by Northwest's own Jerry and Marilyn Fine, was birthed and honed in the lives of our members. Jerry and Marilyn are godly lay leaders who have spent their lives discipling others.

One on One comes out of the crucible of life and involvement in the church. I had the unique opportunity to see the impact of *One on One* in the lives of our members. I have observed person after person discipled with this tool, resulting in lives being dramatically affected.

One on One is what a discipleship program ought to be. It develops people into mature, consistent and balanced Christians. The heart of this discipleship tool is to teach people to walk in an intimate love relationship with Christ through daily Scripture reading and application, prayer and Scripture memory.

One on One is easily transferable. It is so well laid out and the materials so well designed that others can teach them without difficulty. It works well in a small group or one–on–one. People enjoy sharing it with others because of its impact on their own lives.

Our goal was for every church member to complete *One on One*. I have always believed that when people are consistently involved in the Word and in prayer, an unshakable foundation is laid in their lives.

Northwest has been blessed beyond description because of *One on One*. When they developed the study, Jerry and Marilyn could never have known the way God would utilize it. Now *One on One with God* is being used around the world to develop mature disciples. Teens and college students, ministers and laity—all have been strengthened by it. I highly recommend this discipleship tool to you.

Dr. Anthony L. Jordan
Executive Director–Treasurer
Baptist General Convention of Oklahoma

One on One with God:

A ***Path*** that leads to knowing Jesus personally.

A ***Lifestyle*** of walking daily in intimate fellowship with Him.

A ***Tool*** for making disciples and producing disciple makers.

One on One with God
Has Been a Life-Changing Experience for Me

One on One with God has been a life-changing experience for me. Paul's determined purpose to know Jesus deeper, expressed in Philippians 3:10 (AMP), captured my heart and it became my deepest desire and my life's motto. *One on One* was an easy, practical tool to help me learn the discipline of daily investing time in God's Word reading, meditating, studying and memorizing truth. *One on One* helped me cultivate a life of expressing love responses to God in prayer throughout the day. The meditation challenge of the three Ps (ponder, picture, pray) helped me filter the truth of the Scriptures through the prism of my heart and mind. *One on One* has been a great encouragement in my life and an easy tool to pass to others in helping them grow and mature in their faith and walk with the Lord. Sharing with others what the Lord taught me through *One on One* is the greatest joy and blessing!

Adela Constantin, Pharm D.

"For my determined purpose is that I may know Him"

[For my determined purpose is] that I may know Him—
that I may progressively become more deeply and intimately
acquainted with Him, perceiving and recognizing and un-
derstanding [the wonders of His Person] more strongly and
more clearly. And that I may in that same way come to know
the power outflowing from His resurrection [which it ex-
erts over believers]; and that I may so share His sufferings
as to be continually transformed [in spirit into His likeness
even] to His death, [in the hope]

Philippians 3:10 (AMP)

If not here, where?
If not this way, how?
If not now, when?
If not at all, why?

Revised 01/02 Printed 01/05

Notes

INTRODUCTION

Four Parts of Knowing Jesus

Philippians 3:10 (AMP)

My Determined Purpose:

1. To ***progressively become*** more deeply and intimately acquainted with Him.

2. To ***perceive*** and ***recognize*** and ***understand*** the wonders of His person.

3. To ***experience the power*** outflowing from His resurrection. (God's supernatural power)

4. To ***so share His sufferings as to be continually transformed*** in spirit into His likeness.

Sometimes when you are meditating on several truths like this, it helps to meditate on them in reverse order. Try it and see if it helps you. Meditate on the four parts in this order: 4, 3, 2, 1.

Notes

My Commitment to Discipleship Training

1. I will attend all the classes unless prevented for a reason that I know God will approve.

2. I will faithfully do the homework assignments each day.

3. I will enlist one member of this class as my prayer partner.

4. I will contact and pray with my prayer partner each week for the duration of this class.

5. When my prayer partner is absent, I will make contact and seek to encourage him/her.

Signature

Date

Notes

INTRODUCTION

General Lifetime Goals

I. To Know Him:

Reference: Philippians 3:10 (AMP)

> ***[For my determined purpose is] that I may know Him***—that I may progressively become more deeply and intimately acquainted with Him, perceiving and recognizing and understanding [the wonders of His Person] more strongly and more clearly. And that I may in that same way come to know the power outflowing from His resurrection [which it exerts over believers]; and that I may so share His sufferings as to be continually transformed [in spirit into His likeness even] to His death, [in the hope]

II. To Glorify Him:

A. Reference: 1 Corinthians 10:31

> So whether you eat or drink or whatever you do, ***do it all to the glory of God.***

B. Reference: John 17:4 (NKJV)

> ***I have glorified You*** on the earth. I have finished the work which You have given Me to do.

III. To Be Like Him:

As we yield, the Holy Spirit makes the changes:

- ***Our selfish will*** changes to a will that says not my will, but ***"Your will be done."*** Matthew 6:10 (NKJV)

The sermon on the mount.

Notes

INTRODUCTION

- ***Our character*** changes in:

Holiness	1 Peter 1:15–16
Righteousness	Deuteronomy 32:4
Truth	John 1:14; 14:6
Love	1 John 4:7–10
Faithfulness	1 Corinthians 1:9

A. Reference: 2 Corinthians 3:18 (NLT)

> . . . we can be mirrors that brightly reflect the glory of the Lord. ***And as the Spirit of the Lord works within us, we become more and more like Him and reflect His glory even more.***

B. Reference: Romans 12:2 (RSV)

> ***Do not be conformed to this world but be transformed by the renewal of your mind,*** that you may prove what is the will of God, what is good and acceptable and perfect.

C. Reference: Romans 8:29 (RSV)

> For those whom he foreknew he also predestined to ***be conformed to the image of his Son,*** in order that he might be the first–born among many brethren.

Notes

INTRODUCTION

A Look at This Class

I. Motive:

To help Christians walk in intimate fellowship with God through yielded, abiding, committed, disciplined, obedient, loving, trusting, Christ–centered lives.

II. Goal:

A. Encourage.

B. Motivate.

C. Help by equipping and training with:

1. Truth.

2. Lifestyle patterns.

3. Usable and "pass–on–able" tools.

III. Plan:

A. Introduce the subject.

B. Tell them why—Matthew 4:18–19.

C. Show them how—Mark 1:35.

D. Get them started—Matthew 28:19–20.

E. Follow–up—Matthew 26:40, 43, 45; Acts 15:36.

A Verse That Brought Peace

How D. L. Moody helped me.

Rev. J. Wilbur Chapman, D.D.

I will tell you how to be saved, and how you may know you are a Christian. I was studying for the ministry, and I heard that D. L. Moody was to preach in Chicago, and I went down to hear him. I finally got into his after–meeting, and I shall never forget the thrill that went through me, when he came and sat down beside me as an inquirer. He asked me if I was a Christian. I said, "Mr. Moody, I am not sure whether I am a Christian or not."

He asked me some questions, as to whether I was a church member, and I said I was, but was not always sure whether I was a Christian or not. He very kindly took his Bible and opened it at the ***fifth chapter of John, and the twenty–fourth verse,*** which reads as follows: ***"Verily, verily I say unto you, He that heareth my word and believeth on him that sent me hath everlasting life and shall not come into condemnation, but is passed from death unto life."***

Suppose you had read that for the first time, wouldn't you think it was wonderful? I read it through, and he said: ***"Do you believe it?"*** I said, "Yes." ***"Do you accept it?"*** I said, "Yes." "Well, are you a Christian?" "Mr. Moody, I sometimes think I am, and sometimes I am afraid I am not."

He very kindly said, "Read it again."

So I read it again. "Verily, verily I say unto you, He that ***heareth*** my word and ***believeth*** on him that sent me ***hath*** everlasting life, and ***shall not come into condemnation,*** but ***is passed*** from death unto life."

Notes

INTRODUCTION

Then he said, ***"Do you believe it?"*** I said, "Yes." ***"Do you receive Him?"*** I said, "Yes." "Well," he said, "are you a Christian?"

I just started to say over again that sometimes I was afraid I was not, when the only time in all the years I knew him, and loved him, he was sharp with me. He turned on me with his eyes flashing and said, "See here, ***whom are you doubting?"***

Then I saw it for the first time, that ***when I was afraid I was not a Christian, I was doubting God's Word.*** I read it again with my eyes overflowing with tears.

Since that day I have had many sorrows and many joys, but never have I doubted for a moment that I was a Christian, because God said it.

Now what I ask you to do is to plant your feet upon this promise, and say, "Yes, from this moment I know I am a Christian."

A Verse That Brought Peace, the Pocket Testament League Gospel of John. Used by permission.

Notes

INTRODUCTION

Baptism

I. What does this mean?

It means immersion in the water, which is a symbol of the death, burial and resurrection of Jesus. It gives testimony to the fact that I am a follower of Jesus.

II. Why be baptized?

A. Reference: Matthew 28:18–20 (NIV)

> Then Jesus came to them and said, "All authority in heaven and on earth has been given to me. Therefore ***go and make disciples*** of all nations, ***baptizing*** them in the name of the Father and of the Son and of the Holy Spirit, and ***teaching*** them to ***obey everything*** I have commanded you. And surely I am with you always, to the very end of the age."

Answer . . .
Jesus personally instructed His disciples to go do three very important things:

1. Go and make disciples.
2. Baptizing them in the name of the Father and of the Son and of the Holy Spirit.
3. Teach these new disciples to obey everything I have commanded you.

Notes

INTRODUCTION

B. Reference: Luke 6:46 (NLT)

So why do you call me ***"Lord,"*** when you won't ***obey*** me?

Answer . . .
Why do you call me Lord when you won't obey me?

If He is to be Lord, then He must be obeyed.

III. When should I be baptized?

Reference: Matthew 28:18–20 (NIV)

Then Jesus came to them and said, "All authority in heaven and on earth has been given to me. Therefore *go and make disciples* of all nations, ***baptizing*** them in the name of the Father and of the Son and of the Holy Spirit, and ***teaching*** them to ***obey everything*** I have commanded you. And surely I am with you always, to the very end of the age."

Answer . . .
A person should be baptized **A** f **T** e **R** he or she becomes a believer (Christian).

IV. How can I be baptized?

If you have trusted Jesus as your personal Savior, then simply tell the pastor that you want to follow the Lord in baptism.

Three Important Characteristics of True Disciples

True Disciples have many common characteristics. You will find them to be men and women who trust Christ for the strength, and then progressively become:

1. Reference: John 8:31 (AMP)

   So Jesus said to those Jews who had believed in Him, If you abide in My Word—***hold fast to My teachings and live in accordance with them***—you are ***truly*** My disciples.

   Answer . . .
   O B E ___ I ___ N T

2. Reference: Luke 9:23 (NKJV)

   Then He said to them all, If anyone desires to come after Me, let him deny himself, and take up his cross daily, and ***follow*** Me.

   Answer . . .
   F ___ L ___ ___ W ___ R S

3. Reference: Matthew 11:29 (NKJV)

   Take My yoke upon you and ***learn from Me,*** for I am gentle and lowly in heart, and you will find rest for your souls.

   Answer . . .
   L ___ A ___ N ___ R S

Every true disciple of Jesus is trusting in Him, and is committed to applying the truths from God's Word. They are progressively becoming obedient followers and they never stop learning.

Notes

INTRODUCTION

Some Qualities a True Disciple Needs to Cultivate in His Life

1. Reference: Matthew 22:37 (NKJV)

   Jesus said to him, ***"You shall love the Lord your God with all your heart, with all your soul, and with all your mind."***

   Answer . . . Having a heart for the Lord.

2. Reference: Acts 17:11 (RSV)

   Now these Jews were more noble than those in Thessalonica, for they ***received the word with all eagerness,*** examining the scriptures daily to see if these things were so.

   Answer . . . Being open and teachable.

3. Reference: Matthew 11:28–30 (AMP)

   Come to Me, all you who labor and are heavy–laden and over burdened, and I will cause you to rest—I will ease and relieve and refresh your souls. Take My yoke upon you, and ***learn of Me;*** for I am gentle (meek) and humble (lowly) in heart, and you will find rest—relief, ease and refreshment and recreation and blessed quiet—for your souls. For My yoke is wholesome (useful, good)—not harsh, hard, sharp or pressing, but comfortable, gracious and pleasant; and My burden is light and easy to be borne.

   Answer . . . Making oneself available for learning.

4. Reference: Luke 9:23 (NKJV)

   Then He said to them all, If anyone desires to come after Me, let him ***deny himself***, and take up his cross daily, and follow Me.

   Answer . . . Willing to sacrifice to learn.

Sermon or Lesson Notes

Speaker: ______________________ Date: ______________

Location: ______________________ Text: ______________

Title: ____

Listen/Write Down:

- Outline or Main Points
- Scripture References
- Quotes and Illustrations

You may cut here ✂ and/or copy this page.

INTRODUCTION

Review/Apply:
List the truths God has revealed to me through this message that I should apply to my life. **Ponder** and **Picture** these truths and then **Pray** these truths back to God as my personal prayer of **A**doration, **C**onfession, **T**hanksgiving or **S**upplication.

You may cut here ✂ and/or copy this page.

Sermon or Lesson Notes

Speaker: __________ Date: __________

Location: __________ Text: __________

Title: __________

Listen/Write Down:

- Outline or Main Points
- Scripture References
- Quotes and Illustrations

You may cut here ✂ and/or copy this page.

Review/Apply:
List the truths God has revealed to me through this message that I should apply to my life. **Ponder** and **Picture** these truths and then **Pray** these truths back to God as my personal prayer of **A**doration, **C**onfession, **T**hanksgiving or **S**upplication.

You may cut here ✂ and/or copy this page.

Caution . . . . . Caution . . . . . Caution

Don't Be Disillusioned

Becoming a Christian does not make us immune to problems, trials, difficulties, temptations and suffering.

1. Reference: Romans 5:1–4 (LIV)

> So now, since we have been made right in God's sight by ***faith*** in His promises, we can have real ***peace*** with Him because of what Jesus Christ our Lord has done for us. For because of our faith, ***He has*** brought us into this place of highest privilege where we now stand, and we confidently and joyfully look forward to actually ***becoming*** all that ***God*** has had in mind for us to be. We can rejoice, too, when we run into ***problems*** and ***trials*** for we know that they are ***good*** for us—they help us learn to be ***patient.*** And ***patience*** develops ***strength*** of ***character*** in us and helps us ***trust God*** more each time we use it until finally our ***hope*** and ***faith*** are strong and steady.

We are made right in God's sight by **F A ___ T H.**

We have real **P E A ___ E** with God because of what Jesus Christ our Lord has done for us.

We confidently and joyfully look forward to actually **B ___ C O M ___ N G** all that **G ___ D** has in mind for us to be.

Becoming a Christian will not eliminate the **P R ___ B L ___ M S** and **T R ___ A ___ S** in our lives. In fact, they are **G O ___ D** for us, because they help us learn to be **P A ___ I E ___ T.**

Notes

INTRODUCTION

As we become more **P A ___ I E ___ T,** this develops **S T ___ E N ___ T H** of **C H ___ R ___ C T ___ R** in us and helps us **T R ___ S T** God more until finally our **H ___ P E** and **F A ___ T H** are strong and steady.

2. Reference: James 1:2–4 (NLT)

> Dear brothers and sisters, whenever ***trouble*** comes your way, let it be an opportunity for ***joy***. For when your faith is ***tested,*** your ***endurance*** has a chance to grow. So let it grow, for when your ***endurance*** is fully developed, you will be strong in ***character*** and ready for ***anything.***

When the Christian's life is full of **T R ___ U ___ L E,** he is not to get depressed and discouraged, but rather he is to see it as an opportunity for **J ___ Y.**

Why see it as an opportunity for joy when trouble comes your way? Because when trouble comes your way your **E N D ___ ___ A N ___ E** has a chance to grow.

Learning to respond to any situation in life with patient, steadfast endurance seems to be the key to being a Christian fully developed, strong in **C H ___ R ___ C T ___ R,** ready for **A N ___ T H ___ N G.**

3. Reference: James 1:13–14 (NLT)

> And remember, no one who wants to do wrong should ever say, "God is tempting me." ***God*** is never tempted to do wrong, and He ***never tempts anyone*** else either. ***Temptation*** comes from the ***lure*** of our own ***evil*** desires.

Remember this, when someone wants to do wrong it is never **G ___ D** who is **T ___ M P T ___ N G** him.

Notes

INTRODUCTION

We are lured into **T E M ___ T___ T ___ O N** by our own **E ___ I L** desires, therefore don't blame God.

Temptation is not sin, but yielding to temptation is sin.

Notes

INTRODUCTION

The Principle of Displacement

A principle is a God-given truth that becomes a basis or reason prompting faith attitudes and actions.

I. ***The Principle of Displacement*** is found in:

Reference: Philippians 4:8

> Finally, brethren, whatsoever things are ***true,*** whatsoever things are ***honest,*** whatsoever things are ***just,*** whatsoever things are ***pure,*** whatsoever things are ***lovely,*** whatsoever things are of ***good report;*** if there be any ***virtue,*** and if there be any ***praise, think on these things.***

II. By obeying the instruction to ***think on these things,*** we displace the ungodly thoughts and fears that crowd our minds and cause us to live defeated lives. We are actually crowding them out of our minds by filling our minds with pure, godly thoughts of ***love, adoration, praise and thanksgiving.*** We are, in fact,

displacing them.

III. The ***promise from God*** for obeying and practicing this principle is:

Reference: Philippians 4:9

> . . . the God of peace shall be with you.

IV. You will find the ***application of this principle*** very helpful:

A. In cultivating a more loving fellowship with the Lord.

B. When facing trials or temptations.

C. In "bringing into captivity every thought to the obedience of Christ" (2 Corinthians 10:5).

D. In obeying the command, "be transformed by the renewing of your mind . . ." (Romans 12:2 NKJV).

V. Examples of application:

A. Throughout the day ***express your love, adoration, praise and thanksgiving to God.***

B. When facing a trial or temptation, do not focus on the trial or temptation, but rather ***focus on Jesus*** (Hebrews 12:2).

1. Throughout the trial or temptation, ***express your love, adoration, praise and thanksgiving to God.***

2. If the trial demands a response from you, then face the trial ***looking to Jesus*** for deliverance, strength, comfort, needs and direction.

VI. Result of application:

The daily practice of this principle can become a vital part of cultivating a more positive, optimistic, Christ–like lifestyle.

Notes

INTRODUCTION

How to Determine the Quality of My Love

1 Corinthians 13: 4–8

Think through the following statements with a particular person in mind. Rate each statement on the basis of 1–10, with 10 being the highest quality of love. The key word in each statement or question is ***always*** or ***never.***

Score

_____ 1. I am always patient with this person.

_____ 2. I am always kind to this person and find myself searching for opportunities to do good for this person.

_____ 3. I am never envious or jealous of this person.

_____ 4. I am never boastful or arrogant around this person. I am more concerned about his or her thoughts, interests and accomplishments than my own.

_____ 5. I am never rude or unmannerly around this person.

_____ 6. I am never selfish around this person by insisting on my way, demanding my rights or pressing for my selfish aims.

_____ 7. I am never irritable or touchy, quick to take offense or slow to forgive and forget when this person commits an offense against me.

_____ 8. I never rejoice, take pleasure or gloat over the wrong this person does.

_____ 9. I always rejoice when I see truth and justice demonstrated in this person's life.

_____ 10. I always find it easy to overlook this person's faults, and I am unwilling to expose his or her faults to others.

_____ 11. I always find myself eager to believe the best about this person.

_____ 12. I always find myself hoping for the very best for this person regardless of the circumstances.

_____ 13. I have been consistent in demonstrating my love for this person.

_____ 14. My love for this person is growing stronger.

______________ (Total Score) ÷ 1.40 = ______________%

Notes

INTRODUCTION

Daily Commitment Reminder

Since God has good plans for me ***today*** that give me hope and a future. —Jeremiah 29:11 (NIV)

Since God loves me with an everlasting love ***today.*** —Jeremiah 31:3

Since God is the blessed Controller of all things ***today.*** —1 Timothy 6:15 (JBP)

Since God is the love of my life, and He has called me in accordance with His purpose, therefore, He has promised that all things will work together ***today*** for my good. —Romans 8:28

Since I am foreordained to be molded into the image of His Son (Jesus) ***today.*** —Romans 8:29

Since Nothing can separate me from the love of Christ ***today.*** —Romans 8:35, 38–39

Since ***Through Christ,*** I am more than a conqueror ***today*** over trouble, difficulty, persecution, famine, nakedness, peril of my life or the sword of my enemies. —Romans 8:35, 37

Since I can do all things ***through Christ*** who strengthens me ***today.*** —Philippians 4:13

Since I am responsible to bear much fruit ***today,*** and thereby glorify the Father. —John 15:8

Notes

INTRODUCTION

My Daily Commitment Prayer . . .

Lord, *Today* I Commit Myself to:

Know You more deeply and intimately, and to ***keep my eyes fixed on You.***	Phil. 3:10 (AMP) Hebrews 12:2 (NIV)
Trust You with all my heart and not myself, and ***to obey You*** and receive ***Your*** blessing.	Proverbs 3:5 Luke 11:28
Love You with all my heart, soul and mind, and ***to serve You*** with gladness.	Matthew 22:37 Psalm 100:2
Yield to You and ***Your*** control of my life. In fact, right now ***I give You the full control of my life for the rest of today.***	Romans 6:13
Abide in You just as a fruitful branch must continue to abide in (vitally united to) the vine.	John 15:4 (AMP)
Glorify You in every area of my life, including every thought, word, attitude and action.	1 Corinthians 10:31
Guard against the reasons for unfruitfulness: 1. The cares (burdens) of this world. 2. The deceitfulness of riches. 3. The lusts of (for) other things.	Mark 4:19
Reflect You and the fruit of Your Spirit—love, joy, peace, patience, kindness, goodness, faithfulness, gentleness and self–control.	Gal. 5:22–23 (NIV)
Delight in You and ***Your plan*** for my life, and Lord, help me to bring delight to You today.	Psalm 37:4; 40:8
Make disciples as I go.	Matthew 28:19 (NKJV)

Lord, *You know that I cannot live out this commitment today in my own strength. Therefore, please live it out through me today, as I yield to Your control.*

Notes

INTRODUCTION

Encourage Yourself in the Lord

(1 Samuel 30:6; Romans 15:4 NIV)

I. My Lord and Savior is ***Omnipotent (All–Powerful).*** He possesses the ultimate power to meet my every need (Matthew 28:18).

A. I cast ***all my care*** upon my ***Omnipotent (All–Powerful)*** Lord for ***He cares for me*** (1 Peter 5:7) and He will meet my every need (Philippians 4:19), for He says, "Call upon Me in the day of trouble; I will deliver you, and you will glorify Me" (Psalm 50:15 NKJV).

B. My ***Omnipotent (All–Powerful)*** Lord will always draw a line over which the enemy (Satan) cannot step, for "When the enemy shall come in like a flood, ***the Spirit of the Lord shall lift up a standard against him"*** (Isaiah 59:19).

C. My ***Omnipotent (All–Powerful)*** Lord tells me not to fear or be dismayed when the odds against me are great, for ***the battle is not mine, but His*** (2 Chronicles 20:15), and the Lord will fight for me (Exodus 14:14). "Ah, Lord GOD! Behold . . . Your great power . . . There is nothing too hard for You" (Jeremiah 32:17 NKJV).

D. My ***Omnipotent (All–Powerful)*** Lord encourages me ***to fear Him and nothing else*** (Isaiah 8:13 NLT), for He wants to leave me with His peace in exchange for my tormenting fear (John 14:27).

E. My ***Omnipotent (All–Powerful)*** Lord promises me that in the midst of every temptation He will intervene and not allow me to be tempted more than I can stand, but in the face of every temptation, ***He will provide me with a way to escape*** so that ***I do not have to yield*** to that temptation (1 Corinthians 10:13).

Notes

INTRODUCTION

F. My ***Omnipotent (All–Powerful)*** Lord is ***the blessed Controller of all things*** (1 Timothy 6:15 JBP), and as long as I love Him and I am living in accordance with the purpose for which He called me, He has promised that He will not allow anything to touch my life except that which will work together for my good (Romans 8:28).

G. My ***Omnipotent (All–Powerful)*** Lord is ***faithful to exercise His power on my behalf*** (Deuteronomy 7:9), and ". . . The things which are impossible with men are possible with God" (Luke 18:27).

H. My ***Omnipotent (All–Powerful)*** Lord reminds me that "Many are the afflictions of the righteous, ***but the LORD delivereth him (me) out of them all"*** (Psalm 34:19).

I. My ***Omnipotent (All–Powerful)*** Lord ***has even taken the fear and sting out of death,*** for through the Lord Jesus Christ and the resurrection (His and mine), ***I have victory*** (1 Corinthians 15:55, 57).

II. My Lord and Savior is ***Omnipresent (Always Present).*** He is with me every moment of every day (Matthew 28:20).

A. My ***Omnipresent (Always Present)*** Lord has promised that He will ***never leave me nor forsake me*** (Hebrews 13:5).

B. My ***Omnipresent (Always Present)*** Lord tells me not to fear, for ***He will stay with me, strengthen me, help me and uphold me*** (Isaiah 41:10).

C. My ***Omnipresent (Always Present)*** Lord said, "Have I not commanded you? Be strong and of good courage;

do not be afraid, nor be dismayed, ***for the Lord your God is with you wherever you go"*** (Joshua 1:9 NKJV).

D. My ***Omnipresent (Always Present)*** Lord said, "Since you are precious in My sight, since you are honored and I love you . . . ***Do not fear, for I am with you*** . . ." (Isaiah 43:4, 5 NAS).

E. My ***Omnipresent (Always Present)*** Lord is always with me. "Yea, though I walk through the valley of the shadow of death, ***I will fear no evil; for You are with me;*** Your rod and Your staff they comfort me" (Psalm 23:4 NKJV).

III. My Lord and Savior is ***Omniscient (All–Knowing).*** He knows everything, past, present and future (Colossians 2:3).

A. My ***Omniscient (All–Knowing)*** Lord knows everything about me (Psalm 139:1–6), and yet ***He loves me with an everlasting love*** (Jeremiah 31:3).

B. My ***Omniscient (All-Knowing)*** Lord, in all of His wisdom and knowledge, has ordained that various ***trials, tests, hard times and difficult circumstances and situations*** will be a normal part of my Christian life (Romans 5:1–4 LIV; James 1:2–4 NLT; James 1:13–14 NLT). They are the ***channels*** God uses to bring me into the refining fires, where the impurities in my life will be brought to the surface for me to confess and be forgiven (1 John 1:9), and ***in the process I have the opportunity to become transformed in spirit into His likeness*** (Philippians 3:10 AMP).

C. ***My Omniscient (All-Knowing)*** Lord in all His wisdom and knowledge ***has good plans for me.*** These plans include a future for me, and a hope for me,

Notes

INTRODUCTION

therefore I recognize that ***I have a significant place in God's plans*** (Jeremiah 29:11 NIV).

D. ***My Omniscient (All-Knowing)*** Lord knows all of my weaknesses and all of my needs, including my need for love (Psalm 139:1), so He has promised me His everlasting, eternal, unconditional love that is not dependent on my performance (Jeremiah 31:3; Romans 5:6–8). ***God loves me,*** even me, with "His great love," not because of who I am, or what I am, but because of "whose I am" (Acts 27:23; Deuteronomy 7:6–7) and because of His great mercy (Ephesians 2:4).

Beloved Friend,

We are all faced with a series of great opportunities brilliantly disguised as impossible situations.

—Charles Swindoll

Be encouraged! God uses His attributes to bring aid and comfort to those whose hearts are loyal to Him:

- **God's Power** (Omnipotence)
- **God's Presence** (Omnipresence)
- **God's Knowledge** (Omniscience)

You are His prized possession (Deuteronomy 7:6 MOF), and He is watching for opportunities to show Himself strong on your behalf if you are loyal to Him (2 Chronicles 16:9 NKJV).

. . . Blood on Our Hands?

> ". . . I have appointed you a ***watchman*** . . . (if) you do not ***speak to warn*** the wicked from his way, that wicked man shall die in his iniquity (sin), but ***his blood*** will I require from your hand." (Ezekiel 33:1–8 NAS)

> (***Watchman***—one responsible to warn others of approaching danger. ***Warn***—springing from a heart of love, and a spirit of humility. ***Blood on our hands***—a reminder that God will hold Christians responsible and accountable if they do not care enough to share the "good news" about Jesus with the lost.)

Christians, we are the Lord's appointed "watchmen" today.

I. Why is it so urgent for us to share His message?

A. God desires that everyone be saved. He is **"*not willing that any should perish,*** but that all should come to repentance" (2 Peter 3:9).

B. ***Without Jesus there is no hope.*** Jesus said, "I am the way, the truth, and the life. ***No one comes to the Father except through Me"*** (John 14:6 NKJV).

II. What is His message?

All of us have sinned and fallen short of God's desire for us (Romans 3:23). What we have earned and deserve ***(our wages) for our sin is death*** (eternal separation from God). But because of His great love, God has chosen to rescue us by offering us ***a free gift,*** which we neither earn or deserve, and ***that gift is eternal life through Jesus Christ our Lord*** (Romans 6:23).

Why did God do this for you and me?

For God so loved the world ***(you and me)*** that ***He allowed*** His only Son ***(Jesus)*** to take our place on the cross and ***die for our sins,*** and ***whosoever believes in Him (Jesus) will not perish, but will have eternal life*** (John 3:16).

The believing that saves is not just intellectual assent, but it is receiving a person (Jesus Christ) as our personal Lord and Savior, and at that instant we become God's child and join into an eternal relationship with Him (John 1:12).

III. Who are His messengers?

The messengers are ***all those who have believed and received Jesus Christ as their personal Lord and Savior.*** To believers that make up His church, He says, ". . . ***you shall be witnesses to Me*** in Jerusalem, and in all Judea and Samaria, and to the end of the earth" (Acts 1:8 NKJV).

IV. What is His method?

A. Go:

1. So everywhere we ***go*** we ***talk about Christ*** to all who will listen, warning them and teaching them as well as we know how . . . (Colossians 1:28 LIV).
2. As you ***go . . . make disciples*** (Matthew 28:19 NKJV).

B. Send:

> For ***whosoever shall call upon the name of the Lord shall be saved.*** And ***how then shall they call on him*** in whom they have not believed? And ***how shall they believe in him*** of whom they have not heard? And ***how shall they hear*** without a preacher? And ***how shall they preach,*** except they be sent? (Romans 10:13–15)

As we go through each day, we talk about Christ to those we are around and make disciples as we go. And we gladly support with our prayers and our finances those who go where we cannot go or when we cannot go.

V. What is our responsibility?

As we ***pray*** and as we ***go,*** share His message.

A. The Holy Spirit's responsibility is to:

1. ***Illuminate the mind*** of the unbeliever (1 Corinthians 2:12–13).
2. ***Convict the heart*** of the unbeliever (John 16:8).

B. Our responsibility is to:

1. ***Obey***—". . . you shall be witnesses to Me . . ." (Acts 1:8 NKJV).
2. ***Go in Jesus' POWER*** (Matthew 28:18–19).
3. ***Adopt Jesus' PLAN***—as you go, share His message (Matthew 28:19–20).
4. ***Stand on Jesus' PROMISE***—". . . I am with you . . ." (Matthew 28:20).

VI. What is our motivation?

A. Love

There is no greater way to demonstrate our love for God and the lost than to follow the example of our Lord by ***laying down our lives and dying to our selfish desires, so that the lost might be saved.*** "Greater love hath no man than this, that a man lay down his life for his friends" (John 15:13).

B. Concern

The lost are missing the very thing they were created for, and that is ***abundant life.*** There is ***no life apart from Jesus;*** there is ***only an existence.*** For if man can really live apart from Jesus, then Jesus died in vain, for Jesus said, ". . . I am come that they might have life, and that they might have it more ***abundantly (in fullest measure)"*** (John 10:10).

Notes

INTRODUCTION

C. Obedience

How can we call Him Lord and not ***speak to warn*** the lost? "But why do you call Me 'Lord, Lord,' and not do the things which I say?" (Luke 6:46 NKJV).

D. Compassion

The lost are destined to a Christless eternity.

1. ***Hell is a real place of constant and eternal torment.*** It is filled with ***real people*** who may have been our relatives, neighbors, friends or associates. "And these shall go away into ***everlasting punishment:*** but the righteous into life eternal" (Matthew 25:46).

2. ***Hell is a real place where the inhabitants can see into heaven.*** They are in torment, ***forever dying, but never dead.*** "In hell, where he was in torment, he looked up and saw Abraham far away, with Lazarus by his side" (Luke 16:23 NIV).

3. ***Hell is a real place, eternally separated from God,*** His mercy, His followers (Christians) and everything good. ". . . between us and you there is a great gulf fixed, so that those who want to pass from here [heaven] to you cannot, ***nor can those from there [hell] pass to us"*** (Luke 16:26 NKJV).

4. ***Hell is a real place where all requests are denied.*** ". . . send him to my father's house: For I have five brethren; that he may testify unto them, lest they also come into this place of torment [hell]." But ***the request was denied*** (Luke 16:27–31).

E. Accountability

When life on earth has ended, we will be required to stand before the Lord and give account of how we used what God entrusted to us while on earth.

Notes

INTRODUCTION

Surely we will have to account for sharing the most important thing we were given, which was His message. "So then everyone of us shall give account of himself to God" (Romans 14:12).

F. **Repayment of a debt . . .**
Sharing His message is a debt of love I owe. "Yet the proof of God's amazing love is this: that it was while we were sinners that ***Christ died for us***" (Romans 5:8 JPB).

VII. How can we become more effective in sharing His message?

A. ***Memorize verses*** such as Romans 3:23; Romans 6:23; John 3:16: John 1:12; Ephesians 2:8–9.

B. ***Pray*** for opportunities to ***share these verses*** with the lost.

C. ***Ask God to help you think of questions*** that you feel comfortable asking the lost, ***questions that will help create opportunities*** for you ***to share His message.***

Examples:

1. Have you ever had a time when you invited Jesus into your heart as your personal Lord and Savior?
2. Are you a Christian? How did you come to know the Lord? (These questions should be used together)
3. Were you saved in a worship service, or did someone personally lead you to Christ?
4. How did you come to the point of asking Jesus to come into your heart? Tell me about your experience.
5. How old were you when you invited Christ into your life? I would love to hear how it happened.

Notes

INTRODUCTION

D. Consider ***every opportunity to share*** His message as ***a divine encounter, an appointment arranged by God.***

E. ***Don't wait until you think you can make a perfect presentation.*** God usually chooses to show His strength through our weakness.

Several men once told me about a personal friend of theirs who had very little formal education. He had memorized only three scriptures, but in one year he led over 300 people to the Lord. It sounded to me like he was properly responding to the challenge—"So everywhere we go we talk about Christ to all who will listen . . ." (Colossians 1:28 LIV).

It is not how much we know or how eloquently we speak, but how committed and willing we are to share what we know about who we know . . . (Jesus).

List below the ***reasons or excuses that you believe God will approve if you choose not to share*** the message (the good news) everywhere you go with all who will listen.

____

____

____

____

____

____

____

____

____

____

____

____

____

____

Evangelism Challenge for Every Day:

1. ***Be Wise*—"*. . . he who is wise*** captures human lives for God [as a fisher of men]—he gathers and receives them for eternity" (Proverbs 11:30 AMP).
2. ***Be Open—Talk about Jesus*** (Colossians 1:28 NLT). Talk about His Word, who He is, what He means to you, what He has done for you and what He wants to do for them.
3. ***Be Available*—**If you are not already involved in evangelism visitation, start now. If your church offers *Faith, CWT, Evangelism Explosion* or some other type of evangelism training, ***enlist*** as soon as you have finished *One on One with God*. If evangelism training is not offered in your church, ***find someone*** in your church that is actively involved in leading people to the Lord. Ask him/her if they would allow you to make evangelistic visits with him/her for the next four months. ***"Be a vessel . . . for the Master's use, and prepared unto every good work"*** (2 Timothy 2:21). [Note: If just two are visiting together, men should visit with men and women with women, unless the visiting couple are husband and wife or they are both single.]
4. ***Be Bold*—** ". . . for He (God) hath said, I will never leave thee, nor forsake thee. ***So that we may boldly say, The Lord is my helper, and I will not fear what man shall do unto me*"** (Hebrews 13:5–6).
5. ***Be Prepared—The gospel (good news) in a nutshell is simply this:*** Holy God ***came*** to earth as a man (Jesus), ***to die*** on a cruel cross to pay for your sins and mine. After His crucifixion ***He was buried,*** but even death could not defeat Him for ***He arose*** from the grave. ***Now God gives us the victory through our Lord Jesus Christ;*** therefore, we are to be steadfast, unmovable, and always abounding in the work of the Lord (1 Corinthians 15: 3–4, 57–58).

Notes

INTRODUCTION

Where Do You Find Worth and Significance?

Do you sometimes question your worth or significance? What happens when some or all of the world's indicators seem to be telling you that you're a failure and not worth much? Maybe you have just lost your job or experienced the deep hurt of a broken meaningful relationship, or you're just lonely and think that no one cares. Maybe someone is attacking your character or motives. Maybe you have failed in an important assignment or task. Maybe you're discouraged about your appearance, or you just don't see that your life is turning out like you expected. Maybe you can't even put your finger on the cause, but you still feel worthless and insignificant.

On the other hand, maybe at this particular time in your life everything seems to be going your way. You've experienced much success in life and often find yourself being complimented for your great talent, personality, graduation, promotion, fine possessions or appearance. And maybe that has given you a false sense of worth and significance.

There is good news for those who will honestly ask the question: how can I determine my true worth and significance?

A tremendous burden will be lifted, and a spirit of humility will come over us when we fully understand that our worth and significance is solely in our relationship to God through trusting Jesus as our personal Lord and Savior. We must understand that Jesus died on the cross for our sins because God considered that we were significant and worth saving (John 3:16). We were not saved by our performance, nor do we remain saved through our performance (Ephesians 2:8–9).

Notes

INTRODUCTION

To feel that we must perform to earn or deserve worth or significance from God or others is to totally misunderstand what Jesus did for us. It has already been settled. When Jesus took our place on the cross and died for our sins, He proved our worth and significance. Even if others should question our worth and significance, Jesus, who is greater, proved they are wrong by dying for us. Now let's get on with the task that is before us; let's live for Him.

God prefers that our lives not be a performance, but a reflection of Christ at work in us. ". . . we can be mirrors that brightly reflect the glory of the Lord. And as the Spirit of the Lord works within us, we become more and more like Him and reflect His glory even more" (2 Corinthians 3:18 NLT).

The reflection of Jesus at work in us and through us is proof that we belong to Him.

We usually find ourselves trying to excel in the area of our life where we find the greatest significance and worth. Where is your significance? Is it in your spouse, children, home, yard, work, sports, school, intellect, hobby, status, achievement, position, recognition, possessions, money, reputation, popularity, appearance, or is it solely in your relationship to God through trusting Jesus as your personal Lord and Savior? The point is not whether the above things are good or bad, but where you find worth and significance.

We will all live out our frustrated lives running full speed on a treadmill going nowhere until we fully understand that our worth and significance is entirely in our relationship to God through trusting Jesus as our personal Lord and Savior.

The reason we can feel good about ourselves is simply that Jesus died on the cross for our sins because God considered that we were significant and worth saving (John 3:16). And He is not only the judge, but our star witness.

Notes

INTRODUCTION

If you want victory in the area of significance and worth in your life, keep your focus on Jesus and be found faithful, looking to Him (Hebrews 12:2). A true reflection of Jesus will only come from our lives when we:

1. ***Believe***—that our worth and significance is solely based on our relationship to God through trusting Jesus as our personal Lord and Savior (John 3:16; Ephesians 2:8–9).
2. ***Yield***—the control of our lives to Jesus moment by moment (Romans 6:13).
3. ***Abide***—in Jesus throughout each day (John 15:4).
4. ***Apply***—the principles He teaches us in His Word throughout each day (James 1:22) in an effort to bring glory to God (1 Corinthians 10:31).

Read

Notes

Walking In His Word

One on One with God changed our lives! God brought us to this study after many frustrating and unsuccessful attempts to establish a meaningful and productive daily quiet time. For us, *One on One* brought about a lifestyle of daily walking more intimately with Him and living by faith on the promises in His Word. This tool has also effectively equipped us to carry out the "Great Commission" by making disciples and leading others on a path toward a vibrant and fruitful relationship and fellowship with God.

Bob Troester, Government Attorney
Julie Troester, Homemaker

Notes

READ

First Month
Daily Bible Reading Challenge

We encourage you to do your reading ***this first year*** in either the New International Bible, Living Bible or New Living Translation.

Psalm 119

Day of Month	Verses	Day of Month	Verses
1	1–8	16	69–72
2	9–11	17	73–77
3	12–16	18	78–80
4	17–20	19	81–88
5	21–24	20	89–96
6	25–27	21	97–104
7	28–32	22	105–112
8	33–35	23	113–120
9	36–42	24	121–128
10	43–48	25	129–136
11	49–52	26	137–144
12	53–56	27	145–152
13	57–61	28	153–160
14	62–64	29	161–168
15	65–68	30	169–176

Notes

R
E
A
D

Daily Bible Reading Challenge

Second Month:

1. Read the ***New Testament*** section in the "Daily Bible Reading Calendar." (Pages 51–62)

*2. Read ***one chapter in Proverbs.***

Third Month:

1. Read the ***New Testament*** section in the "Daily Bible Reading Calendar." (Pages 51–62)
2. Read the ***Old Testament–I*** section in the "Daily Bible Reading Calendar." (Pages 51–62)

*3 Read ***one chapter in Proverbs.***

Fourth Month And Thereafter:

1. Read the ***New Testament*** section in the "Daily Bible Reading Calendar." (Pages 51–62)
2. Read the ***Old Testament–I*** section in the "Daily Bible Reading Calendar." (Pages 51–62)
3. Read the ***Old Testament–II*** section in the "Daily Bible Reading Calendar." (Pages 51–62)

*4. Read ***one chapter in Proverbs.***

* Each day in Proverbs read the chapter that has the same number as that day's date—the first day of the month read the first chapter, and the second day of the month read the second chapter, etc.

Notes

The Daily Bible Reading Calendar

JANUARY

And beginning with Moses and with all the prophets, He explained to them the things concerning Himself in all the Scriptures (Luke 24:27).

	Old Testament I	Old Testament II	New Testament
1	❑ Gen. 1:1 to 2:3	❑ Job 1:1 to 2:10	❑ Matt. 1
2	❑ Gen. 2:4–25	❑ Job 2:11 to 3:26	❑ Matt. 2
3	❑ Gen. 3	❑ Job 4, 5	❑ Matt. 3
4	❑ Gen. 4, 5	❑ Job 6, 7	❑ Matt. 4
5	❑ Gen. 6:1 to 7:10	❑ Job 8	❑ Matt. 5:1–20
6	❑ Gen. 7:11 to 8:19	❑ Job 9, 10	❑ Matt. 5:21–48
7	❑ Gen. 8:20 to 9:29	❑ Job 11, 12	❑ Matt. 6:1–18
8	❑ Gen . 10:1 to 11:26	❑ Job 13, 14	❑ Matt. 6:19 to 7:6
9	❑ Gen. 11:27 to 12:20	❑ Job 15	❑ Matt. 7:7–29
10	❑ Gen. 13, 14	❑ Job 16, 17	❑ Matt. 8:1–27
11	❑ Gen. 15, 16	❑ Job 18, 19	❑ Matt. 8:28 to 9:17
12	❑ Gen. 17	❑ Job 20	❑ Matt. 9:18–38
13	❑ Gen. 18	❑ Job 21	❑ Matt. 10:1–25
14	❑ Gen. 19	❑ Job 22	❑ Matt. 10:26 to 11:1
15	❑ Gen. 20, 21	❑ Job 23, 24	❑ Matt. 11:2–30
16	❑ Gen. 22	❑ Job 25, 26, 27	❑ Matt. 12:1–21
17	❑ Gen. 23	❑ Job 28	❑ Matt. 12:22–50
18	❑ Gen. 24	❑ Job 29, 30	❑ Matt. 13:1–23
19	❑ Gen. 25	❑ Job 31	❑ Matt. 13:24–43
20	❑ Gen. 26	❑ Job 32, 33	❑ Matt. 13:44 to 14:13
21	❑ Gen. 27	❑ Job 34, 35	❑ Matt. 14:14–36
22	❑ Gen. 28	❑ Job 36, 37	❑ Matt. 15:1–28
23	❑ Gen. 29	❑ Job 38, 39	❑ Matt. 15:29 to 16:12
24	❑ Gen. 30	❑ Job 40, 41	❑ Matt. 16:13 to 17:13
25	❑ Gen. 31	❑ Job 42	❑ Matt. 17:14 to 18:14
26	❑ Gen. 32:1 to 33:16	❑ Psalms 1, 2, 3	❑ Matt. 18:15–35
27	❑ Gen. 33:17 to 34:31	❑ Psalms 4. 5, 6	❑ Matt. 19:1–15
28	❑ Gen. 35	❑ Psalms 7, 8	❑ Matt. 19:16 to 20:16
29	❑ Gen. 36	❑ Psalms 9, 10	❑ Matt. 20:17–34
30	❑ Gen. 37	❑ Psalms 11, 12, 13, 14	❑ Matt. 21:1–32
31	❑ Gen. 38	❑ Psalms 15, 16	❑ Matt. 21:33 to 22:14

Notes

READ

The Daily Bible Reading Calendar

FEBRUARY

The law of the Lord is perfect, restoring the soul: the testimony of the Lord is sure, making wise the simple (Psalm 19:7).

	Old Testament I	Old Testament II	New Testament
1	❑ Gen. 39	❑ Psalm 17	❑ Matt. 22:15–46
2	❑ Gen. 40	❑ Psalm 18:1–29	❑ Matt. 23
3	❑ Gen. 41:1–49	❑ Psalm 18:30–50	❑ Matt. 24:1–28
4	❑ Gen. 41:50 to 42:38	❑ Psalm 19	❑ Matt. 24:29–51
5	❑ Gen. 43	❑ Psalms 20, 21	❑ Matt. 25:1–30
6	❑ Gen. 44	❑ Psalm 22	❑ Matt. 25:31 to 26:2
7	❑ Gen. 45	❑ Psalms 23, 24	❑ Matt. 26:3–30
8	❑ Gen. 46:1 lo 47:26	❑ Psalm 25	❑ Matt. 26:31–57
9	❑ Gen. 47:27 to 48:22	❑ Psalms 26, 27	❑ Matt. 26:58–75
10	❑ Gen. 49	❑ Psalms 28, 29	❑ Matt. 27:1–26
11	❑ Gen. 50	❑ Psalm 30	❑ Matt. 27:27–44
12	❑ Exod. 1:1 to 2:22	❑ Psalm 31	❑ Matt. 27:45–68
13	❑ Exod. 2:23 to 3:22	❑ Psalms 32, 33	❑ Matt. 28
14	❑ Exod. 4	❑ Psalm 34	❑ Acts 1
15	❑ Exod. 5:1 to 6:12	❑ Psalms 35, 36	❑ Acts 2:1–21
16	❑ Exod. 6:13 to 7:25	❑ Psalm 37	❑ Acts 2:22–47
17	❑ Exod. 8	❑ Psalms 38, 39	❑ Acts 3
18	❑ Exod. 9	❑ Psalms 40, 41	❑ Acts 4:1–31
19	❑ Exod. 10	❑ Psalms 42, 43	❑ Acts 4:32 to 5:11
20	❑ Exod. 11:1 to 12:20	❑ Psalm 44	❑ Acts 5:12–42
21	❑ Exod. 12:21–51	❑ Psalms 45, 46	❑ Acts 6
22	❑ Exod. 13:1 to 14:4	❑ Psalms 47, 48	❑ Acts 7:1–29
23	❑ Exod. 14:5–31	❑ Psalms 49, 50	❑ Acls 7:30 to 8:4
24	❑ Exod. 15	❑ Psalm 51	❑ Acts 8:5–40
25	❑ Exod. 16	❑ Psalms 52, 53, 54	❑ Acts 9:1–31
26	❑ Exod. 17	❑ Psalm 55	❑ Acts 9:32–43
27	❑ Exod. 18	❑ Psalms 56, 57	❑ Acts 10:1–23
28	❑ Exod. 19	❑ Psalms 58, 59	❑ Acts 10:24–48

Notes

R
E
A
D

The Daily Bible Reading Calendar

MARCH

How can a young man keep his way pure? By keeping it according to Thy word (Psalm 119:9).

	Old Testament I	Old Testament II	New Testament
1	❑ Exod. 20	❑ Psalms 60, 61	❑ Acts 11:1–18
2	❑ Exod. 21	❑ Psalms 62, 63	❑ Acts 11:19–30
3	❑ Exod. 22:1 to 23:9	❑ Psalms 64, 65	❑ Acts 12
4	❑ Exod. 23:10–33	❑ Psalms 66, 67	❑ Acts 13:1–25
5	❑ Exod. 24	❑ Psalm 68	❑ Acts 13:26–52
6	❑ Exod. 25	❑ Psalm 69	❑ Acts 14
7	❑ Exod. 26:1–30	❑ Psalms 70, 71	❑ Acts 15:1–21
8	❑ Exod. 26:31 to 27:19	❑ Psalm 72	❑ Acts 15:22–35
9	❑ Exod. 27:20 to 28:14	❑ Psalm 73	❑ Acts 15:36 to 16:15
10	❑ Exod. 28:15–43	❑ Psalms 74, 75	❑ Acts 16:16–40
11	❑ Exod. 29:1–37	❑ Psalms 76, 77	❑ Acts 17:1–15
12	❑ Exod. 29:38 to 30:10	❑ Psalm 78:1–31	❑ Acts 17:16–34
13	❑ Exod. 30:11–38	❑ Psalm 78:32–72	❑ Acts 18:1–22
14	❑ Exod. 31	❑ Psalms 79, 80	❑ Acts 18:23 to 19:20
15	❑ Exod. 32	❑ Psalms 81, 82	❑ Acts 19:21–41
16	❑ Exod. 33:1 to 34:3	❑ Psalms 83, 84	❑ Acts 20:1–16
17	❑ Exod. 34:4–35	❑ Psalms 85, 86	❑ Acts 20:17–38
18	❑ Exod. 35	❑ Psalms 87, 88	❑ Acts 21:1–16
19	❑ Exod. 36	❑ Psalm 89:1–18	❑ Acts 21:17–40
20	❑ Exod. 37	❑ Psalm 89:19–52	❑ Acts 22:1–21
21	❑ Exod. 38	❑ Psalms 90, 91	❑ Acts 22:22 to 23:11
22	❑ Exod. 39	❑ Psalms 92, 93	❑ Acts 23:12–35
23	❑ Exod. 40	❑ Psalms 94, 95	❑ Acts 24
24	❑ Lev. 1	❑ Psalms 96, 97, 98	❑ Acts 25:1–22
25	❑ Lev. 2	❑ Psalms 99, 100, 101	❑ Acts 25:23 to 26:11
26	❑ Lev. 3	❑ Psalm 102	❑ Acts 26:12–32
27	❑ Lev. 4:1–26	❑ Psalm 103	❑ Acts 27:1–26
28	❑ Lev. 4:27 to 5:13	❑ Psalm 104	❑ Acts 27:27 to 28:10
29	❑ Lev. 5:14 to 6:7	❑ Psalm 105	❑ Acts 28:11–31
30	❑ Lev. 6:8 to 7:10	❑ Psalm 106	❑ Mark 1:1–20
31	❑ Lev. 7:11–38	❑ Psalm 107	❑ Mark 1:21–45

Notes

The Daily Bible Reading Calendar

APRIL

But these have been written that you may believe that Jesus is the Christ, the Son of God; and that believing you may have life in His name (John 20:31).

	Old Testament I	Old Testament II	New Testament
1	❑ Lev. 8	❑ Psalm 108	❑ Mark 2:1–22
2	❑ Lev. 9	❑ Psalm 109	❑ Mark 2:23 to 3:12
3	❑ Lev. 10	❑ Psalms 110, 111	❑ Mark 3:13–35
4	❑ Lev. 11	❑ Psalms 112, 113, 114	❑ Mark 4:1–20
5	❑ Lev. 12:1 to 13:23	❑ Psalms 115, 116	❑ Mark 4:21–41
6	❑ Lev. 13:24–59	❑ Psalms 117, 118	❑ Mark 5:1–20
7	❑ Lev. 14:1–32	❑ Psalm 119:1–40	❑ Mark 5:21–43
8	❑ Lev. 14:33–57	❑ Psalm 119:41–72	❑ Mark 6:1–29
9	❑ Lev. 15	❑ Psalm 119:73–112	❑ Mark 6:30–56
10	❑ Lev. 16	❑ Psalm 119:113–144	❑ Mark 7:1–23
11	❑ Lev. 17, 18	❑ Psalm 119:145–176	❑ Mark 7:24 to 8:10
12	❑ Lev. 19, 20	❑ Psalms 120 to 123	❑ Mark 8:11–26
13	❑ Lev. 21	❑ Psalms 124 to 127	❑ Mark 8:27 to 9:13
14	❑ Lev. 22	❑ Psalms 128 to 131	❑ Mark 9:14–32
15	❑ Lev. 23:1–22	❑ Psalms 132, 133	❑ Mark 9:33–50
16	❑ Lev. 23:23–44	❑ Psalms 134, 135	❑ Mark 10:1–31
17	❑ Lev. 24	❑ Psalms 136, 137	❑ Mark 10:32–52
18	❑ Lev. 25	❑ Psalms 138, 139	❑ Mark 11:1–26
19	❑ Lev. 26	❑ Psalms 140, 141	❑ Mark 11:27 to 12:17
20	❑ Lev. 27	❑ Psalms 142, 143	❑ Mark 12:18–44
21	❑ Num. 1	❑ Psalms 144, 145	❑ Mark 13
22	❑ Num. 2	❑ Psalms 146, 147	❑ Mark 14:1–26
23	❑ Num. 3	❑ Psalms 148 to 150	❑ Mark 14:27–52
24	❑ Num. 4	❑ Prov. 1	❑ Mark 14:53–72
25	❑ Num. 5	❑ Prov. 2	❑ Mark 15:1–23
26	❑ Num. 6	❑ Prov. 3	❑ Mark 15:24–47
27	❑ Num. 7	❑ Prov. 4	❑ Mark 16
28	❑ Num. 8	❑ Prov. 5:1 to 6:19	❑ 1 Pet. 1:1– 12
29	❑ Num. 9:1 to 10:10	❑ Prov. 6:20 to 7:27	❑ 1 Pet. 1:13 to 2:10
30	❑ Num. 10:11 to 11:3	❑ Prov. 8	❑ 1 Pet. 2:11 to 3:7

READ

Notes

READ

The Daily Bible Reading Calendar

MAY

Like newborn babes, long for the pure milk of the word, that by it you may grow in respect to salvation (1 Peter 2:2).

	Old Testament I	Old Testament II	New Testament
1	❑ Num. 11:4–35	❑ Prov. 9	❑ 1 Pet. 3:8–22
2	❑ Num. 12, 13	❑ Prov. 10	❑ 1 Pet. 4
3	❑ Num. 14	❑ Prov. 11	❑ 1 Pet. 5
4	❑ Num. 15	❑ Prov. 12	❑ 2 Pet. 1
5	❑ Num. 16:1–40	❑ Prov. 13	❑ 2 Pet. 2
6	❑ Num. 16:41 to 17:13	❑ Prov. 14	❑ 2 Pet. 3
7	❑ Num. 18	❑ Prov. 15	❑ James 1
8	❑ Num. 19	❑ Prov. 16	❑ James 2
9	❑ Num. 20	❑ Prov. 17	❑ James 3
10	❑ Num. 21	❑ Prov. 18	❑ James 4
11	❑ Num. 22:1–38	❑ Prov. 19	❑ James 5
12	❑ Num. 22:39 to 23:26	❑ Prov. 20:1 to 21:11	❑ Jude
13	❑ Num. 23:27 to 24:25	❑ Prov. 21:12 to 22:16	❑ Luke 1:1–25
14	❑ Num.25:1 to 26:51	❑ Prov. 22:17 to 23:11	❑ Luke 1:26–56
15	❑ Num. 26:52 to 27:23	❑ Prov. 23:12–35	❑ Luke 1:57–80
16	❑ Num. 28	❑ Prov. 24	❑ Luke 2:1–21
17	❑ Num. 29	❑ Prov. 25:1 to 26:12	❑ Luke 2:22–52
18	❑ Num. 30, 31	❑ Prov. 26:13 to 27:27	❑ Luke 3
19	❑ Num. 32	❑ Prov. 28	❑ Luke 4:1–15
20	❑ Num. 33	❑ Prov. 29	❑ Luke 4:16–44
21	❑ Num. 34:1 to 35:8	❑ Prov. 30	❑ Luke 5:1–16
22	❑ Num. 35:9 to 36:13	❑ Prov. 31	❑ Luke 5:17–39
23	❑ Deut. 1	❑ Eccl. 1:1 to 2:10	❑ Luke 6:1–19
24	❑ Deut. 2	❑ Eccl. 2:11 to 3:15	❑ Luke 6:20–49
25	❑ Deut. 3	❑ Eccl. 3:16 to 4:16	❑ Luke 7:1–29
26	❑ Deut. 4	❑ Eccl. 5, 6	❑ Luke 7:30–50
27	❑ Deut. 5	❑ Eccl. 7	❑ Luke 8:1–21
28	❑ Deut. 6:1 to 7:10	❑ Eccl. 8:1 to 9:10	❑ Luke 8:22–39
29	❑ Deut. 7:11 to 8:20	❑ Eccl. 9:11 to 10:20	❑ Luke 8:40–56
30	❑ Deut. 9:1 to 10:11	❑ Eccl. 11, 12	❑ Luke 9:1–17
31	❑ Deut. 10:12 to 11:32	❑ Song 1:1 to 2:7	❑ Luke 9:18–36

Notes

R
E
A
D

The Daily Bible Reading Calendar

JUNE

The gospel of God, which He promised beforehand through His prophets in the holy Scriptures (Romans 1:1, 2).

	Old Testament I	Old Testament II	New Testament
1	❑ Deut. 12	❑ Song 2:8 to 3:5	❑ Luke 9:37–62
2	❑ Deut. 13:1 to 14:21	❑ Song 3:6 to 5:1	❑ Luke 10:1–24
3	❑ Deut. 14:22 to 15:23	❑ Song 5:2 to 6:9	❑ Luke 10:25–42
4	❑ Deut. 16	❑ Song 6:10 to 8:14	❑ Luke 11:1–13
5	❑ Deut. 17:1 to 18:8	❑ Obadiah	❑ Luke 11:14–36
6	❑ Deut. 18:9 to 19:21	❑ Joel 1	❑ Luke 11:37–54
7	❑ Deut. 20, 21	❑ Joel 2	❑ Luke 12:1–21
8	❑ Deut. 22:1 to 23:8	❑ Joel 3	❑ Luke 12:22–40
9	❑ Deut. 23:9 to 24:22	❑ Jonah 1, 2	❑ Luke 12:41–59
10	❑ Deut. 25:1 to 26:15	❑ Jonah 3, 4	❑ Luke 13:1–21
11	❑ Deut. 26:16 to 27:26	❑ Amos 1, 2	❑ Luke 13:22–35
12	❑ Deut. 28:1–37	❑ Amos 3, 4	❑ Luke 14:1–24
13	❑ Deut. 28:38–68	❑ Amos 5, 6	❑ Luke 14:25 to 15:10
14	❑ Deut. 29	❑ Amos 7, 8	❑ Luke 15:11–32
15	❑ Deut. 30:1 to 31:13	❑ Amos 9	❑ Luke 16
16	❑ Deut. 31:14 to 32:14	❑ Hosea 1:1 to 2:1	❑ Luke 17:1–19
17	❑ Deut. 32:15–52	❑ Hosea 2:2 to 3:5	❑ Luke 17:20 to 18:14
18	❑ Deut. 33	❑ Hosea 4:1 to 6:3	❑ Luke 18:15–43
19	❑ Deut. 34	❑ Hosea 6:4 to 7:16	❑ Luke 19:1–28
20	❑ Joshua 1	❑ Hosea 8, 9	❑ Luke 19:29–48
21	❑ Joshua 2	❑ Hosea 10:1 to 11:11	❑ Luke 20:1–19
22	❑ Joshua 3	❑ Hosea 11:12 to 14:9	❑ Luke 20:20 to 21:4
23	❑ Joshua 4:1 to 5:12	❑ Isa. 1	❑ Luke 21:5–38
24	❑ Joshua 5:13 to 6:27	❑ Isa. 2	❑ Luke 22:1–30
25	❑ Joshua 7	❑ Isa. 3, 4	❑ Luke 22:31–53
26	❑ Joshua 8	❑ Isa. 5	❑ Luke 22:54 to 23:12
27	❑ Joshua 9	❑ Isa. 6	❑ Luke 23:13–46
28	❑ Joshua 10	❑ Isa. 7:1 to 8:4	❑ Luke 23:47 to 24:12
29	❑ Joshua 11, 12	❑ Isa. 8:5 to 9:7	❑ Luke 24:13–53
30	❑ Joshua 13	❑ Isa. 9:8 to 10:5	❑ 1 Thess. 1

Notes

The Daily Bible Reading Calendar

JULY

All scripture is inspired by God and profitable for teaching, for reproof, for correction, for training in righteousness (2 Timothy 3:16).

	Old Testament I	Old Testament II	New Testament
1	❑ Joshua 14, 15	❑ Isa. 10:6–34	❑ 1 Thess. 2:1–16
2	❑ Joshua 16, 17	❑ Isa. 11, 12	❑ 1 Thess. 2:17 to 3:13
3	❑ Joshua 18, 19	❑ Isa. 13	❑ 1 Thess. 4
4	❑ Joshua 20, 21	❑ Isa. 14	❑ 1 Thess. 5
5	❑ Joshua 22	❑ Isa. 15, 16	❑ 2 Thess. 1
6	❑ Joshua 23	❑ Isa. 17, 18	❑ 2 Thess. 2
7	❑ Joshua 24	❑ Isa. 19, 20	❑ 2 Thess. 3
8	❑ Judges 1:1 to 2:5	❑ Isa. 21:1 to 22:14	❑ 1 Cor. 1
9	❑ Judges 2:6 to 3:4	❑ Isa. 22:15 to 23:18	❑ 1 Cor. 2
10	❑ Judges 3:5–31	❑ Isa. 24	❑ 1 Cor. 3
11	❑ Judges 4	❑ Isa. 25	❑ 1 Cor. 4
12	❑ Judges 5	❑ Isa. 26	❑ 1 Cor. 5
13	❑ Judges 6	❑ Isa. 27	❑ 1 Cor. 6
14	❑ Judges 7	❑ Isa. 28	❑ 1 Cor. 7
15	❑ Judges 8	❑ Isa. 29	❑ 1 Cor. 8
16	❑ Judges 9:1 to 10:5	❑ Isa. 30	❑ 1 Cor. 9:1–23
17	❑ Judges 10:6 to 11:28	❑ Isa. 31, 32	❑ 1 Cor. 9:24 to 10:14
18	❑ Judges 11:29 to 12:15	❑ Isa. 33	❑ 1 Cor. 10:15 to 11:1
19	❑ Judges 13	❑ Isa. 34, 35	❑ 1 Cor. 11:2–34
20	❑ Judges 14, 15	❑ Isa. 36:1 to 37:7	❑ 1 Cor. 12
21	❑ Judges 16	❑ Isa. 37:8–38	❑ 1 Cor. 13
22	❑ Judges 17, 18	❑ Isa. 38, 39	❑ 1 Cor. 14
23	❑ Judges 19	❑ Isa. 40	❑ 1 Cor. 15:1–34
24	❑ Judges 20	❑ Isa. 41:1–20	❑ 1 Cor. 15:35–58
25	❑ Judges 21	❑ Isa. 41:21 to 42:21	❑ 1 Cor. 16
26	❑ Ruth 1	❑ Isa. 42:22 to 43:10	❑ 2 Cor. 1
27	❑ Ruth 2	❑ Isa. 43:11 to 44:5	❑ 2 Cor. 2
28	❑ Ruth 3, 4	❑ Isa. 44:6–23	❑ 2 Cor. 3:1 to 4:6
29	❑ 1 Sam. 1	❑ Isa. 44:24 to 45:8	❑ 2 Cor. 4:7 to 5:10
30	❑ 1 Sam. 2	❑ Isa. 45:9–25	❑ 2 Cor. 5:11 to 6:10
31	❑ 1 Sam. 3	❑ Isa. 46	❑ 2 Cor. 6:11 to 7:16

READ

Notes

READ

The Daily Bible Reading Calendar

AUGUST

But know this first of all, that no prophecy of Scripture is a matter of one's own interpretation, for no prophecy was ever made by an act of human will, but men moved by the Holy Spirit spoke from God (2 Peter 1:20, 21).

	Old Testament I	Old Testament II	New Testament
1	❑ 1 Sam. 4, 5	❑ Isa. 47	❑ 2 Cor. 8
2	❑ 1 Sam. 6, 7	❑ Isa. 48	❑ 2 Cor. 9
3	❑ 1 Sam. 8:1 to 9:14	❑ Isa. 49	❑ 2 Cor. 10
4	❑ 1 Sam. 9:15 to 10:27	❑ Isa. 50:1 to 51:8	❑ 2 Cor. 11
5	❑ 1 Sam. 11, 12	❑ Isa. 51:9–23	❑ 2 Cor. 12:1–13
6	❑ 1 Sam. 13	❑ Isa. 52:1–12	❑ 2 Cor. 12:14 to 13:14
7	❑ 1 Sam. 14	❑ Isa. 52:13 to 53:12	❑ Rom. 1:1–16
8	❑ 1 Sam. 15	❑ Isa. 54	❑ Rom. 1:17–32
9	❑ 1 Sam. 16	❑ Isa. 55:1 to 56:8	❑ Rom. 2
10	❑ 1 Sam. 17:1–31	❑ Isa. 56:9 to 57:21	❑ Rom. 3
11	❑ 1 Sam. 17:32–58	❑ Isa. 58	❑ Rom. 4:1–22
12	❑ 1 Sam. 18:1 to 19:7	❑ Isa. 59	❑ Rom. 4:23 to 5:11
13	❑ 1 Sam. 19:8 to 20:42	❑ Isa. 60	❑ Rom. 5:12–21
14	❑ 1 Sam. 21, 22	❑ Isa. 61	❑ Rom. 6:1–14
15	❑ 1 Sam. 23, 24	❑ Isa. 62:1 to 63:14	❑ Rom. 6:15 to 7:6
16	❑ 1 Sam. 25	❑ Isa. 63:15 to 64:12	❑ Rom. 7:7–25
17	❑ 1 Sam. 26, 27	❑ Isa. 65	❑ Rom. 8:1–17
18	❑ 1 Sam. 28, 29	❑ Isa. 66	❑ Rom. 8:18–39
19	❑ 1 Sam. 30, 31	❑ Micah 1, 2	❑ Rom. 9:1–29
20	❑ 2 Sam. 1	❑ Micah 3:1 to 4:8	❑ Rom. 9:30 to 10:21
21	❑ 2 Sam. 2	❑ Micah 4:9 to 5:15	❑ Rom. 11:1–15
22	❑ 2 Sam. 3	❑ Micah 6	❑ Rom. 11:16–36
23	❑ 2 Sam. 4, 5	❑ Micah 7	❑ Rom. 12
24	❑ 2 Sam. 6	❑ Nahum 1	❑ Rom. 13
25	❑ 2 Sam. 7	❑ Nahum 2, 3	❑ Rom. 14:1–18
26	❑ 2 Sam. 8, 9	❑ Hab. 1	❑ Rom. 14:19 to 15:13
27	❑ 2 Sam. 10, 11	❑ Hab. 2	❑ Rom. 15:14–33
28	❑ 2 Sam. 12	❑ Hab. 3	❑ Rom. 16
29	❑ 2 Sam. 13	❑ Zeph. 1	❑ Gal. 1
30	❑ 2 Sam. 14	❑ Zeph. 2	❑ Gal. 2
31	❑ 2 Sam. 15	❑ Zeph. 3	❑ Gal. 3:1–14

Notes

The Daily Bible Reading Calendar

SEPTEMBER

The Spirit of the Lord spoke by me, and His word was on my tongue (2 Samuel 23:2).

	Old Testament I	Old Testament II	New Testament
1	❑ 2 Sam. 16, 17	❑ Jer. 1	❑ Gal. 3:15–29
2	❑ 2 Sam. 18:1 to 19:8	❑ Jer. 2	❑ Gal. 4:1–20
3	❑ 2 Sam. 19:9–43	❑ Jer. 3:1 to 4:2	❑ Gal. 4:21 to 5:9
4	❑ 2 Sam. 20	❑ Jer. 4:3–31	❑ Gal. 5:10–26
5	❑ 2 Sam. 21	❑ Jer. 5	❑ Gal. 6
6	❑ 2 Sam. 22	❑ Jer. 6	❑ Eph. 1:1–14
7	❑ 2 Sam. 23	❑ Jer. 7	❑ Eph. 1:15 to 2:10
8	❑ 2 Sam. 24	❑ Jer. 8	❑ Eph. 2:11–22
9	❑ 1 Kings 1	❑ Jer. 9	❑ Eph. 3
10	❑ 1 Kings 2	❑ Jer. 10	❑ Eph. 4:1–16
11	❑ 1 Kings 3	❑ Jer. 11	❑ Eph. 4:17–32
12	❑ 1 Kings 4, 5	❑ Jer. 12	❑ Eph. 5:1–21
13	❑ 1 Kings 6	❑ Jer. 13	❑ Eph. 5:22 to 6:9
14	❑ 1 Kings 7	❑ Jer. 14	❑ Eph. 6:10–24
15	❑ 1 Kings 8:1–30	❑ Jer. 15	❑ Phil. 1:1–20
16	❑ 1 Kings 8:31–66	❑ Jer. 16	❑ Phil. 1:21 to 2:11
17	❑ 1 Kings 9	❑ Jer. 17	❑ Phil. 2:12–30
18	❑ 1 Kings 10	❑ Jer. 18	❑ Phil. 3:1 to 4:1
19	❑ 1 Kings 11	❑ Jer. 19, 20	❑ Phil. 4:2–23
20	❑ 1 Kings 12:1–24	❑ Jer. 22	❑ Col. 1:1–20
21	❑ 1 Kings 12:25 to 13:32	❑ Jer. 23	❑ Col. 1:21 to 2:7
22	❑ 1 Kings 13:33 to 14:31	❑ Jer. 25	❑ Col. 2:8 to 3:4
23	❑ 1 Kings 15:1–32	❑ Jer. 26	❑ Col. 3:5 to 4:1
24	❑ 1 Kings 15:33 to 16:34	❑ Jer. 35	❑ Col. 4:2–18
25	❑ 1 Kings 17	❑ Jer. 36, 45	❑ Philemon
26	❑ 1 Kings 18	❑ Jer. 46, 47	❑ Heb. 1
27	❑ 1 Kings 19	❑ Jer. 48	❑ Heb. 2
28	❑ 1 Kings 20	❑ Jer. 49	❑ Heb. 3
29	❑ 1 Kings 21	❑ Jer. 50	❑ Heb. 4:1–13
30	❑ 1 Kings 22	❑ Jer. 51:1–24	❑ Heb. 4:14 to 5:10

READ

Notes

READ

The Daily Bible Reading Calendar

OCTOBER

The Scripture had to be fulfilled, which the Holy Spirit foretold by the mouth of David concerning Judas (Acts 1:16).

	Old Testament I	Old Testament II	New Testament
1	❑ 2 Kings 1	❑ Jer. 51:25–64	❑ Heb. 5:11 to 6:20
2	❑ 2 Kings 2	❑ Jer. 24, 29	❑ Heb. 7
3	❑ 2 Kings 3	❑ Jer. 30	❑ Heb. 8
4	❑ 2 Kings 4	❑ Jer. 31	❑ Heb. 9:1–14
5	❑ 2 Kings 5	❑ Jer. 27, 28	❑ Heb. 9:15–28
6	❑ 2 Kings 6:1–23	❑ Jer. 21, 34	❑ Heb. 10:1–18
7	❑ 2 Kings 6:24 to 7:20	❑ Jer. 37	❑ Heb. 10:19–39
8	❑ 2 Kings 8	❑ Jer. 32:1–25	❑ Heb. 11:1–16
9	❑ 2 Kings 9	❑ Jer. 32:26–44	❑ Heb. 11:17–40
10	❑ 2 Kings 10	❑ Jer. 33	❑ Heb. 12:1–17
11	❑ 2 Kings 11, 12	❑ Jer. 38	❑ Heb. 12:18 to 13:6
12	❑ 2 Kings 13:1 to 14:22	❑ Jer. 39	❑ Heb. 13:7–25
13	❑ 2 Kings 14:23 to 15:31	❑ Jer. 40	❑ Titus 1:1 to 2:8
14	❑ 2 Kings 15:32 to 16:20	❑ Jer. 41	❑ Titus 2:9 to 3:15
15	❑ 2 Kings 17	❑ Jer. 42, 43	❑ 1 Tim. 1
16	❑ 2 Kings 18	❑ Jer. 44	❑ 1 Tim. 2
17	❑ 2 Kings 19	❑ Jer. 52	❑ 1 Tim. 3
18	❑ 2 Kings 20:1 to 21:18	❑ Lam. 1	❑ 1 Tim. 4
19	❑ 2 Kings 21:19 to 22:20	❑ Lam. 2	❑ 1 Tim. 5
20	❑ 2 Kings 23	❑ Lam. 3	❑ 1 Tim. 6
21	❑ 2 Kings 24	❑ Lam. 4, 5	❑ 2 Tim. 1
22	❑ 2 Kings 25	❑ Ezek. 1	❑ 2 Tim. 2
23	❑ 1 Chron. 1	❑ Ezek. 2:1 to 3:15	❑ 2 Tim. 3
24	❑ 1 Chron. 2	❑ Ezek. 3:16 to 4:17	❑ 2 Tim. 4
25	❑ 1 Chron. 3:1 to 4:23	❑ Ezek. 5, 6	❑ John 1:1–18
26	❑ 1 Chron. 4:24 to 5:26	❑ Ezek. 7	❑ John 1:19–51
27	❑ 1 Chron. 6	❑ Ezek. 8, 9	❑ John 2:1–22
28	❑ 1 Chron. 7	❑ Ezek. 10	❑ John 2:23 to 3:21
29	❑ 1 Chron. 8, 9	❑ Ezek. 11	❑ John 3:22–36
30	❑ 1 Chron. 10, 11	❑ Ezek. 12	❑ John 4:1–30
31	❑ 1 Chron. 12	❑ Ezek. 13	❑ John 4:31–54

Notes

The Daily Bible Reading Calendar

NOVEMBER

But the things which God announced beforehand by the mouth of all the prophets, that His Christ should suffer, He has thus fulfilled (Acts 3:18).

	Old Testament I	Old Testament II	New Testament
1	❑ 1 Chron. 13, 14	❑ Ezek. 14, 15	❑ John 5:1–23
2	❑ 1 Chron. 15	❑ Ezek. 16:1–34	❑ John 5:24–47
3	❑ 1 Chron. 16	❑ Ezek. 16:35–63	❑ John 6:1–21
4	❑ 1 Chron. 17, 18	❑ Ezek. 17	❑ John 6:22–40
5	❑ 1 Chron. 19, 20	❑ Ezek. 18, 19	❑ John 6:41 to 7:1
6	❑ 1 Chron. 21	❑ Ezek. 20:1–44	❑ John 7:2–30
7	❑ 1 Chron. 22, 23	❑ Ezek. 20:45 to 21:32	❑ John 7:31 to 8:11
8	❑ 1 Chron. 24, 25	❑ Ezek. 22	❑ John 8:12–30
9	❑ 1 Chron. 26, 27	❑ Ezek. 23	❑ John 8:31–59
10	❑ 1 Chron. 28	❑ Ezek. 24, 25	❑ John 9:1–17
11	❑ 1 Chron. 29	❑ Ezek. 26	❑ John 9:18–38
12	❑ 2 Chron. 1, 2	❑ Ezek. 27	❑ John 9:39 to 10:18
13	❑ 2 Chron. 3, 4	❑ Ezek. 28	❑ John 10:19–42
14	❑ 2 Chron. 5:1 to 6:11	❑ Ezek. 29:1 to 30:19	❑ John 11:1–27
15	❑ 2 Chron. 6:12–42	❑ Ezek. 30:20 to 31:18	❑ John 11:28–54
16	❑ 2 Chron. 7	❑ Ezek. 32	❑ John 11:55 to 12:19
17	❑ 2 Chron. 8, 9	❑ Ezek. 33	❑ John 12:20–50
18	❑ 2 Chron. 10, 11	❑ Ezek. 34	❑ John 13:1–30
19	❑ 2 Chron. 12, 13	❑ Ezek. 35:1 to 36:15	❑ John 13:31 to 14:14
20	❑ 2 Chron. 14, 15	❑ Ezek. 36:16–38	❑ John 14:15–31
21	❑ 2 Chron. 16, 17	❑ Ezek. 37	❑ John 15:1–16
22	❑ 2 Chron. 18, 19	❑ Ezek. 38	❑ John 15:17 to 16:15
23	❑ 2 Chron. 20	❑ Ezek. 39	❑ John 16:16–33
24	❑ 2 Chron. 21, 22	❑ Ezek. 40	❑ John 17
25	❑ 2 Chron. 23, 24	❑ Ezek. 41	❑ John 18:1–27
26	❑ 2 Chron. 25	❑ Ezek. 42	❑ John 18:28 to 19:16
27	❑ 2 Chron. 26	❑ Ezek. 43	❑ John 19:17–42
28	❑ 2 Chron. 27, 28	❑ Ezek. 44	❑ John 20
29	❑ 2 Chron. 29	❑ Ezek. 45	❑ John 21
30	❑ 2 Chron. 30	❑ Ezek. 46	❑ 1 John 1

READ

Notes

READ

The Daily Bible Reading Calendar

DECEMBER

Now He said to them, "These are My words which I spoke to you while I was still with you, that all things which are written about Me in the Law of Moses and the Prophets and the Psalms must be fufilled" (Luke 24:44).

	Old Testament I	Old Testament II	New Testament
1	❑ 2 Chron. 31	❑ Ezek. 47	❑ 1 John 2:1–17
2	❑ 2 Chron. 32	❑ Ezek. 48	❑ 1 John 2:18–29
3	❑ 2 Chron. 33	❑ Dan. 1	❑ 1 John 3
4	❑ 2 Chron. 34	❑ Dan. 2:1–23	❑ 1 John 4
5	❑ 2 Chron. 35	❑ Dan. 2:24–49	❑ 1 John 5
6	❑ 2 Chron. 36	❑ Dan. 3	❑ 2 John
7	❑ Ezra 1, 2	❑ Dan. 4	❑ 3 John
8	❑ Ezra 3, 4	❑ Dan. 5	❑ Rev. 1
9	❑ Ezra 5	❑ Dan. 6	❑ Rev. 2:1–17
10	❑ Ezra 6	❑ Dan. 7	❑ Rev. 2:18 to 3:6
11	❑ Ezra 7	❑ Dan. 8	❑ Rev. 3:7–22
12	❑ Ezra 8	❑ Dan. 9	❑ Rev. 4
13	❑ Ezra 9	❑ Dan. 10	❑ Rev. 5
14	❑ Ezra 10	❑ Dan. 11:1–20	❑ Rev. 6
15	❑ Neh. 1, 2	❑ Dan. 11:21–45	❑ Rev. 7
16	❑ Neh. 3	❑ Dan. 12	❑ Rev. 8
17	❑ Neh. 4	❑ Haggai 1	❑ Rev. 9
18	❑ Neh. 5	❑ Haggai 2	❑ Rev. 10
19	❑ Neh. 6	❑ Zech. 1	❑ Rev. 11
20	❑ Neh. 7	❑ Zech. 2, 3	❑ Rev. 12
21	❑ Neh. 8	❑ Zech. 4	❑ Rev. 13
22	❑ Neh. 9	❑ Zech. 5, 6	❑ Rev. 14
23	❑ Neh. 10, 11	❑ Zech. 7	❑ Rev. 15
24	❑ Neh. 12	❑ Zech. 8	❑ Rev. 16
25	❑ Neh. 13	❑ Zech. 9, 10	❑ Rev. 17
26	❑ Esther 1	❑ Zech. 11	❑ Rev. 18
27	❑ Esther 2	❑ Zech. 12:1 to 13:6	❑ Rev. 19:1–10
28	❑ Esther 3, 4	❑ Zech. 13:7 to 14:21	❑ Rev. 19:11 to 20:6
29	❑ Esther 5, 6	❑ Malachi 1:1 to 2:9	❑ Rev. 20:7 to 21:8
30	❑ Esther 7, 8	❑ Malachi 2:10 to 3:6	❑ Rev. 21:9 to 22:5
31	❑ Esther 9, 10	❑ Malachi 3:7 to 4:6	❑ Rev. 22:6–21

Notes

Note Helps

1. ***Adoration*—Is there anything in this passage that reminds me to express my adoration to the Lord for some part of His moral character?**

    Holiness
    Righteousness
    Truth
    Love
    Faithfulness

2. ***Confession*—**Is there anything in this passage that calls to my attention a sin or sins I need to confess?

3. ***Thanksgiving*—**Is there anything in this passage that encourages me to express thanksgiving to God?

4. ***Supplication*—**Is there anything in this passage that reminds me of a need I have or needs of others that I should ask God to meet?

READ

READ

Daily Bible Reading (DBR) Notes

Date	Reference	Note
9/1/00	Psalm 119:2	"Happy are all who search for God and always do His Will."
9/2	" :11	Storing God's Word in my heart can hold me back from sin.
9/3	" : 12 & 15	Lord, teach me your Word and help me to meditate on it and give it my full respect.
9/4	" :18	"Open my eyes to see wonderful things in your Word."
	" :19	Lord, thank you for being my map, my chart, and my guide in this journey through life.

Sample

You may cut here ✂ and/or copy this page.

READ

Daily Bible Reading (DBR) Notes

Date	Reference	Note
5/9/06	Psalm 119: 1-8	Happy are those who search for Him with all the heart!
" "	" 9-11	How stay pure? Obey Him! Hide His word in your heart,
" "	" 12-16	We must study His commandments and reflect on His ways.
" "	" 17-20	Open my eyes to see the truths of your law. I need the guidance of your commands.
" "	" 21-24	People scorn me but I will meditate on your principles.
" "	" 25-27	Help me understand!
" "	" 28-32	encourage me, let me know your law, I am faithful, Help me
5/10/06 "	" 33-35	Happiness is found along the Lords path.
" "	" 36-42	Don't let me focus on worthless things, your law is what I want.
" "	" 43-48	I <u>honor</u> and <u>love</u> your commandments!
5/11/06 "	" 49-52	Your laws comfort me. Your promaces comfort me.
5/13/06 "	" 53-56	Christian Music!
" "	" 59	Ponder the direction of my life then turn it over to God

Daily Bible Reading (DBR) Notes

Date	Reference	Note
5/15/06	Psalms 119:63	I should be friends with anyone who fears God.
"	" "68	God is Good!!
5/16/06	" "71	The suffering you sent me has been good for me.
5/17/06	" "76	His promise to comfort me!
5/18/06	" "80	Help me be blameless.
5/20/06	" "92	Keep your eyes on the Lord and everything will be OK. He sustains you with joy.
"	" "96	Perfection has its limets but not his commandments I am not Perfect!!
5/23/06	" "105	"Your word is a lamp for my feet and a light for my path" Guide me with your word!
"	" "114	I wish I could shair this verse with some people cus they have no hope.
5/24/06	" "124	even though we are his servents he can deal with us with unfailing love! Amazing!
5/29/06	" "166	I long for your salvation. How awsome!

READ

You may cut here ✂ and/or copy this page.

You may cut here ✄ and/or copy this page.

Daily Bible Reading (DBR) Notes

READ

Date	Reference	Note
	Luke 3:11	That is a great concept
		give to the poor because
		if you have 2 coats,
		they have none, give
		one to them.
	Luke 3:21-22	~~Was~~ The Holy Spirit
		decended on Jesus
		when He was baptised...
		Was he not truly the
		Son of God untill He was
		baptised?

R E A D

Daily Bible Reading (DBR) Notes

Date	Reference	Note
		Psalm 4:3 The lord will
		answer when I call
		Psalm 9:9 Lord is shelter
		for the opressed and
		refage in times of trouble
		Psalm 18:2 - find protection
		He is my shield
		Psaml 23:1 He is every
		thing I need
		Psalm 32:8 I will watch
		over you and guide you
		Psalm 50:15 He will rescue
		you and give you
		glory
		Proverbes 3:5 He will
		direct your paths

You may cut here ✂ and/or copy this page.

You may cut here ✂ and/or copy this page.

Daily Bible Reading (DBR) Notes

Date	Reference	Note

READ

Daily Bible Reading (DBR) Notes

Date	Reference	Note

You may cut here ✂ and/or copy this page.

You may cut here ✂ and/or copy this page.

Daily Bible Reading (DBR) Notes

Date	Reference	Note

READ

Daily Bible Reading (DBR) Notes

Date	Reference	Note

You may cut here ✂ and/or copy this page.

Meditate

Notes

MEDITATE

God Transformed Our Hearts & Minds

We had ceased attending church during the first two years of our marriage, and our hearts had grown cold and hard towards each other and towards people. Through *One on One with God* the Lord really began to transform our hearts and our minds. Over the next few years we found ourselves intersecting in a number of lives and showing them how to be true disciples of Jesus. Steve invited four medical students to join him in a *One on One with God* group near his work. Within a few sessions, it was exciting to see the Spirit of the Lord at work within these students as they were overcome with humility. God captured their hearts. Now, God is advancing His kingdom as they make disciples.

Steve Sezate, Research Assistant
Karen Sezate, Physician Assistant

Notes

Meditation Challenge

God speaks to us in the Old Testament and the New Testament to teach us the importance of meditation and how to meditate.

The word ***mind*** in Matthew 22:37 and Mark 12:30 comes from the Greek word "dianoia," which means ***deep thought*** or ***imagination***. (*Strong's Exhaustive Concordance of the Bible, Greek Dictionary of the New Testament,* page 22, number 1271.)

The word ***meditate*** in Joshua 1:8, Psalm 1:2; 63:6 and 77:12 comes from the Hebrew word "hagah," which means ***to ponder or imagine*** and ***to speak or talk.*** (*Strong's Exhaustive Concordance of the Bible, Hebrew and Chaldee Dictionary,* page 32, number 1897.)

The word ***meditate*** in Psalm 119:15, 23, 48, 78 and 148 comes from the Hebrew word "siyach," which means ***to ponder*** and ***pray.*** (*Strong's Exhaustive Concordance of the Bible, Hebrew and Chaldee Dictionary,* page 115, number 7878.)

The word ***meditation*** in Psalm 119:97 and 99 comes from the Hebrew word "siychah," which means ***reflection, devotion*** and ***prayer.*** (*Strong's Exhaustive Concordance of the Bible, Hebrew and Chaldee Dictionary,* page 115, number 7881.)

Jesus often spoke in parables. Sometimes He used these common life stories and illustrations to communicate spiritual truths by using words to paint pictures in the minds of those He taught. The Holy Spirit does the same for us today as we read and meditate on the written Word, the Bible.

Notes

Therefore, when God tells me to meditate He is telling me to do three things:

1. **Ponder—*seriously think*** about this truth. What is God saying to me personally?
2. **Picture—*form a mental picture*** of this truth. ***See*** myself in the ***picture*** and ***imagine*** my response.
3. **Pray—*talk to God*** about applying this truth. Pray this truth back to God as my personal prayer of **A**doration, **C**onfession, **T**hanksgiving or **S**upplication.

M E D I T A T E

Psalm 63 is a good example of how David practiced these three parts of meditation:

1. In verse 1, David begins by ***talking to God.*** **(Pray)**
2. In verse 2, David says, "to ***see*** thy power and thy glory," and "as I have ***seen*** thee":

   a) ***See*** is from the Hebrew word "raah," which means ***gaze or view.*** (*Strong's Exhaustive Concordance of the Bible, Hebrew and Chaldee Dictionary,* page 106, number 7200.) **(Picture)**

   b) ***Seen*** is from the Hebrew word "chazah," which means ***to mentally gaze at.*** (*Strong's Exhaustive Concordance of the Bible, Hebrew and Chaldee Dictionary,* page 38, number 2372.) **(Picture)**
3. From the text it is obvious that David had been ***pondering, seriously thinking about,*** the goodness of God. **(Ponder)**

Meditation involves **3 Ps:**

Ponder.

Picture.

Pray.

Notes

Helps on How to Picture and Pray in Meditation:

- Put myself in the picture. Ask the following questions: Who is in the picture with me and what are we doing? Is God in the picture? Is God speaking to me in the picture?

- Three ways to picture and pray in meditation:

  1. As I read God's Word, ***I imagine that I am a painter,*** painting the scene about which I am reading. When the picture I see is complete, I talk to God (pray) about what He is saying to me in the picture.

  2. As I read God's Word, ***I imagine the Lord sitting across a narrow table, directly in front of me.*** He looks me in the eye, calls me by name, and says, "Listen closely, this is personal and just for you. I want you to apply this truth in your life." The picture I see is the Lord speaking directly to me. I share with the group what He is saying to me, and then talk to the Lord (pray) about the truth He wants me to apply to my life.

  3. As I read God's Word, ***the picture I see is a daily situation (a modern day experience),*** in which I can apply the truth He is sharing with me. Then I talk to the Lord (pray) about applying the truth.

Note:

Meditation is not
emptying my mind
but filling my mind with
a picture of God's truth
and how it applies to me.

Notes

Now let's practice these **3** parts of meditation:

Read Matthew 27:33–39, then:

1. **Ponder—*seriously think*** about this truth. What is God saying to me personally?
2. **Picture—*form a mental picture*** of this truth. ***See*** myself in the picture and ***imagine*** my response.
3. **Pray—*talk to God*** about applying this truth. ***Pray this truth back*** to God as my personal prayer of **A**doration, **C**onfession, **T**hanksgiving or **S**upplication.

M E D I T A T E

Read Matthew 14:24–33, then:

1. **Ponder—*seriously think*** about this truth. What is God saying to me personally?
2. **Picture—*form a mental picture*** of this truth. ***See*** myself in the picture and ***imagine*** my response.
3. **Pray—*talk to God*** about applying this truth. ***Pray this truth back*** to God as my personal prayer of **A**doration, **C**onfession, **T**hanksgiving or **S**upplication.

In the coming weeks we will ***Meditate***
(Ponder, Picture and Pray) on the following:

1. The ***notes we make*** while reading God's Word.
2. The ***scriptures we memorize.***
3. The ***thoughts we write down*** while studying God's Word.
4. Our ***sermon or lesson notes.***

Prayer

Notes

P R A Y E R

Jesus Became Lord of My Life

Fourteen years ago in *One on One with God,* I learned how to allow Jesus to be Lord of my life. Year after year as I have discipled others using *One on One,* the Lord has made my prayer life vibrant, challenged my love for others, the lost (including my enemies), love for myself and my love toward my spouse. It has taught me how to live a victorious Christian life by allowing the Holy Spirit to have control of my life and abiding in Jesus one day at a time. And it has given me a tool for fulfilling the "Great Commission."

Cindy Ackerman, Homemaker, Medical Transcriptionist

Notes

Read!

Prayer Challenge

Daily . . . . . Hourly . . . . . Moment By Moment

1. Reference: Ephesians 6:18 (NLT)

   Pray at all times and on every occasion in the power of the Holy Spirit. Stay alert and be persistent in your prayers for all Christians everywhere.

2. Reference: 1 Thessalonians 5:16–18 (RSV)

   Rejoice always, ***pray constantly,*** give thanks in all circumstances; for this is the will of God in Christ Jesus for you.

Prayer is not to be confined to once a day. Rather, it is cultivating natural loving responses to God throughout each day. ***True prayer becomes a lifestyle,*** not an occasional thing.

Notes

PRAYER

Prayer Challenge
(continued)

The following acrostic is offered merely as a guide to help you cultivate an active prayer life.

Adoration

Yours, O Lord, is the greatness, the power, the glory, the victory, and the majesty. Everything in the heavens and on earth is yours, O Lord, and this is your kingdom. ***We adore you*** as the one who is over all things. 1 Chronicles 29:11 (NLT)

Confession

But if we ***confess*** our sins to Him, He is faithful and just to forgive us and to cleanse us from every wrong. 1 John 1:9 (NLT)

Thanksgiving

Always and for everything giving thanks in the name of our Lord Jesus Christ to God the Father. Ephesians 5:20 (RSV)

Supplication (humble asking)

Ask, and it will be given to you; seek, and you will find; knock, and it will be opened to you. Matthew 7:7 (NKJV)

Daily Prayer Reminder

Adoration . . . . Confession . . . . Thanksgiving . . . . Supplication

From: 3/11/06 To: ________________

In prayers of supplication, how long do we pray about a matter? We pray until God gives us peace in our hearts. In the garden Jesus prayed three times about the same thing (Matthew 26:36–46 NKJV). Why didn't He just pray once, or why not twenty times? I am convinced that ***He prayed until He had peace in His heart.*** He received that peace because of His confidence in the Father, which He demonstrated by saying, "Nevertheless not as I will, but as You will . . .Your will be done."

> Now this is the ***confidence that we have in Him,*** that if we ask anything according to His will, He hears us. And if we know that He hears us, whatever we ask, we know that we have the petitions that we have asked of Him. (1 John 5:14–15 NKJV)

One more word before you begin to pray:

> The Spirit helps us in our weakness. We do not know what we ought to pray, but ***the Spirit himself intercedes for us*** with groans that words cannot express. (Romans 8:26 NIV)

Person/Subject	Need	Date I received peace
FAMILY MEMBERS:		
Mother	Sickness	3/15/06
FRIENDS:		
Valerie McLure	Sicknes	~~3/22/06~~
PEOPLE I AM DISCIPLING OR HAVE DISCIPLED:		
Valerie Angell	Recieve God	

You may cut here ✂ and/or copy this page.

PRAYER

Person/Subject	Need	Date I received peace
NON-CHRISTIANS:		
VOCATIONAL CHRISTIAN WORKERS:		
MISSIONARIES:		
Sydney	$ for winel river	
GOVERNMENT LEADERS:		
OTHERS WITH PHYSICAL, SPIRITUAL, MENTAL OR EMOTIONAL NEEDS:		
MY PHYSICAL, SPIRITUAL, MENTAL OR EMOTIONAL NEEDS; MY RESPONSIBILITIES AND PROJECTS:		

PRAYER

You may cut here ✂ and/or copy this page.

You may cut here ✂ and/or copy this page.

Daily Prayer Reminder

Adoration . . . . Confession . . . . Thanksgiving . . . . Supplication

From: ________________ To: ________________

In prayers of supplication, how long do we pray about a matter? We pray until God gives us peace in our hearts. In the garden Jesus prayed three times about the same thing (Matthew 26:36–46 NKJV). Why didn't He just pray once, or why not twenty times? I am convinced that ***He prayed until He had peace in His heart.*** He received that peace because of His confidence in the Father, which He demonstrated by saying, "Nevertheless not as I will, but as You will . . .Your will be done."

> Now this is the ***confidence that we have in Him,*** that if we ask anything according to His will, He hears us. And if we know that He hears us, whatever we ask, we know that we have the petitions that we have asked of Him. (1 John 5:14–15 NKJV)

One more word before you begin to pray:

> The Spirit helps us in our weakness. We do not know what we ought to pray, but ***the Spirit himself intercedes for us*** with groans that words cannot express. (Romans 8:26 NIV)

PRAYER

Person/Subject	Need	Date I received peace
FAMILY MEMBERS:		
FRIENDS:		
PEOPLE I AM DISCIPLING OR HAVE DISCIPLED:		

Person/Subject	Need	Date I received peace
NON-CHRISTIANS:		
VOCATIONAL CHRISTIAN WORKERS:		
MISSIONARIES:		
GOVERNMENT LEADERS:		
OTHERS WITH PHYSICAL, SPIRITUAL, MENTAL OR EMOTIONAL NEEDS:		
MY PHYSICAL, SPIRITUAL, MENTAL OR EMOTIONAL NEEDS; MY RESPONSIBILITIES AND PROJECTS:		

PRAYER

You may cut here ✂ and/or copy this page.

Study

Notes

Life Is Not About Me, It Is About Jesus

When I was fifteen years old, my *One on One with God* instructor challenged me with this: Do you think you (or anyone else) could do a better job of running your life than Jesus Christ? The answer is obvious, but I wasn't sure I wanted to give that control to anyone. Through *One on One with God* and reading God's Word, I became convicted and convinced of this, and my perspective on life changed dramatically. Life is not about me; it's about *Him!*

My wife and I have led several people through *One on One with God*. One couple had the privilege of leading their three daughters to the Lord while going through *One on One with God* themselves. It is exciting to see those we've discipled investing time in God's Word and prayer and faithfully serving God year after year. It is very humbling to think God might have somehow, in a small way, used us to impact someone else's life for eternity.

Tom Banks, IT Consultant
Becky Banks, Homemaker, Teacher

Notes

Daily Bible Study Challenge

Instructions:

1. Read the assigned section carefully.
2. Fill in the blanks.
3. Pause to ***meditate*** (**Ponder**, **Picture** and **Pray**) on each thought expressed in the assigned section, especially where you filled in the blanks.

Assignment:	**Prepare for Session #:**
1, 2 and 3	No Bible Study assignment.
4	Pages 91–97
5	Pages 98–106
6	Pages 107–119
7	Pages 120–128
8	Pages 129–135
9	Pages 136–147
10	Pages 148–154
11	Pages 155–164
12	Pages 165–170
13	Pages 171–178
14	Pages 179–186
15	Pages 187–191

Notes

Assignment after Session 15:

Begin your own personal **Bible Study.** In the **"Study"** section of your notebook, after the Study on Love, you will find pages that contain the following information which will be helpful to you as you launch out into your own personal **Bible Study:**

1. ***"Daily Bible Study Challenge"*** — after Session 15 (Page 192)

2. ***"Helps in Personal Bible Study"*** (Page 193)

3. ***"Methods of Bible Study"*** (Pages 194–227)

4. ***"Helpful Bible Study Tools"*** (Pages 228–232)

STUDY

Notes

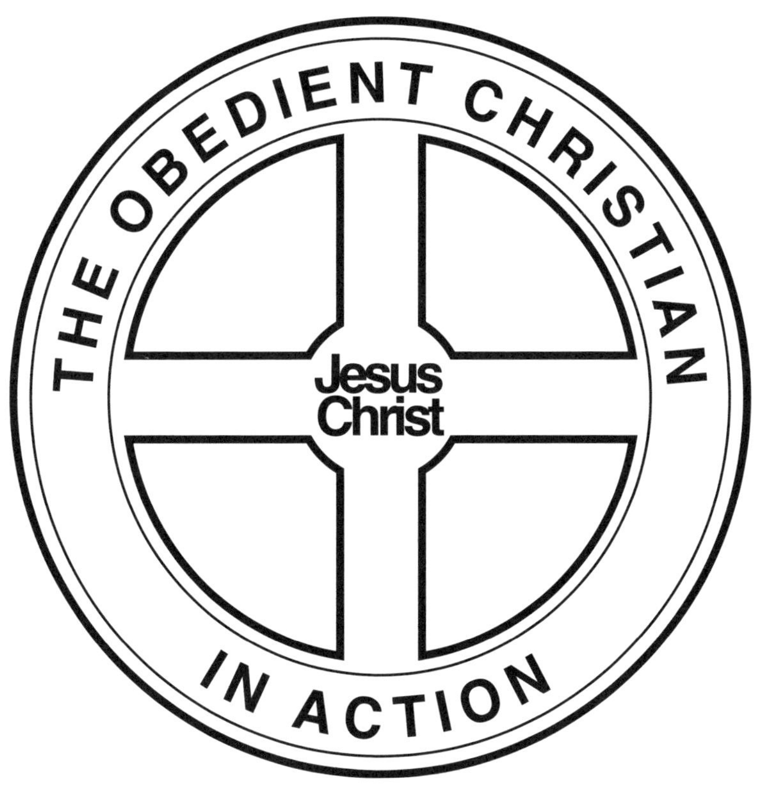

STUDY

The key to living a victorious, Spirit–filled Christian life is Jesus Christ as the center and Lord of all we do. With Christ in control, life is balanced and effective. The Wheel illustrates this Christ–centered life.

> Just as the driving force in a wheel comes from the hub; so ***the power to live the Christian life comes from Jesus Christ, the center.*** He lives in us in the person of the Holy Spirit, whose express purpose is to glorify Christ. The rim represents the Christian responding to Christ's Lordship through wholehearted, day–by–day obedience to Him.

Notes

Allowing Jesus Christ to Be the Center and Lord of My Life

I. What does this mean?

It simply means that I voluntarily yield to God's control of my life, and no longer desire to independently run my own life. Self is taken off the throne in my heart, and Jesus is crowned Lord.

II. Why allow Jesus Christ to be the center and Lord of my life?

Search the following scriptures for answers, and fill in the blanks.

A. Reference: Colossians 1:15–19 (LIV)

> Christ is the exact likeness of the unseen God. He existed before God made anything at all, and, in fact, ***Christ Himself is the Creator who made everything in heaven and earth,*** the things we can see and the things we can't; the spirit world with its kings and kingdoms, its rulers and authorities; all were made by Christ for His own ***use*** and ***glory.*** He was before all else began and ***it is His power that holds everything together.*** He is the Head of the body made up of His people—that is, His church—which He began; and He is the Leader of all those who arise from the dead, so that ***He is first in everything;*** for God wanted all of Himself to be in His Son.

Jesus Christ is the central figure in all creation. Everything made in heaven and earth was made by ____________ for His own ____________ and ____________. It is His ____________ that holds everything together. He is ____________ in everything. Everything in creation revolves around Christ. Therefore, He should be allowed to be the center and Lord of my life around which everything in my life revolves.

STUDY

Notes

B. Reference: Revelation 4:11 (NKJV)

> You are ***worthy,*** O Lord, to receive glory and honor and power; for You ***created*** all things, and by Your will they exist and were created.

Jesus is ______________ of being the center and Lord of my life since I was ______________ by Him.

C. Reference: 1 Corinthians 6:19–20 (NLT)

> Or don't you know that your body is the temple of the Holy Spirit, who lives in you and was given to you by God? ***You do not belong to yourself,*** for God ***bought*** you with a high price. So you must honor God with your body.

Jesus should be allowed to be the center and Lord of my life, not only because He created me, but also because He ______________ me at a great price. The price He paid was the sacrifice of His own life on the cross.

D. Reference: John 10:10 (NKJV)

> The thief does not come except to steal, and to kill, and to destroy. I have come that they may have life, and that they may have it more ***abundantly.***

Jesus should be allowed to be the center and Lord of my life, because I want to experience ______________ life.

E. Jesus should be allowed to be the center and Lord of my life, because He is the key to living a victorious, Spirit–filled Christian life (Galatians 2:20, Romans 6:13 and John 15:4).

Notes

F. Jesus should be allowed to be the center and Lord of my life, because ***He can and will do a better job of running my life than I can.***

Three things convince me that ***Jesus can and will do a better job of running my life than I can:***

1. Reference: Isaiah 45:22 (NKJV)

    Look to Me, and be saved, all you ends of the earth! For ***I am God,*** and there is no other.

    Reference: John 10:30 (NKJV)

    I and My Father are one.

    God claims to be God, and Jesus claims that He and the Father are one. Some say that Jesus was a good man, but not God the Son. Jesus is either a lunatic, or an impostor, or ***He is God,*** for He could not be a good man and lie about who he was. ***He is God.*** As God, He knows everything, and is always with us, ready and able to guide and direct our lives.

    Jesus can and will do a better job of running my life than I can because:

    He is God.

2. Reference: Matthew 28:18 (NKJV)

    And Jesus came and spoke to them, saying, ***"All authority has been given to Me in heaven and on earth."***

    Reference: Ephesians 1:19–22 (NKJV)

    And what is the ***exceeding greatness of His power*** toward us who believe, according to the working of ***His mighty power*** which He worked

STUDY

in Christ when He raised Him from the dead and seated Him at His right hand in the heavenly places, ***far above all principality and power and might and dominion, and every name that is named, not only in this age but also in that which is to come.*** And ***He has put all things under His feet,*** and gave Him to be head over all things to the church.

Reference: Mark 4:39–41 (NKJV)

Then He arose and rebuked the wind, and said to the sea, "Peace, be still!" And the wind ceased and there was a great calm. But He said to them, "Why are you so fearful? How is it that you have no faith?" And they feared exceedingly, and said to one another, "Who can this be, that ***even the wind and the sea obey Him!"***

Reference: 1 Timothy 6:15 (JBP)

God, who is the blessed ***Controller of all things,*** the King over all kings and the Master of all masters. . . .

Jesus can and will do a better job of running my life than I can because:

He is the powerful
C O N_t_R_O_L_l_E R of all things.

3. Reference: Deuteronomy 7:9 (NKJV)

Therefore know that the LORD your God, He is God, the ***faithful*** God who keeps covenant and mercy for a thousand generations with those who love Him and keep His commandments.

Reference: 1 Corinthians 1:9 (NKJV)

God is ***faithful,*** by whom you were called into the fellowship of His Son, Jesus Christ our Lord.

STUDY

Notes

Reference: 2 Thessalonians 3:3

> But the Lord is **faithful**, who shall establish you, and keep you from evil.

Reference: 2 Timothy 2:13 (NKJV)

> If we are faithless, He remains **faithful**; He cannot deny Himself.

I can trust Jesus to do a better job of running my life than I can because:

He is faithful.

Summary:
These three things convince me that Jesus can and will do a better job of running my life than I can:

Jesus is:

1. **G_O_D.**

2. The powerful **CON_t_R_o_L_l_ER** of all things.

3. **FA_i_THF_u_L.**

STUDY

Notes

Summary

Why should I allow Jesus Christ to be the center and Lord of my life?

A. ***Jesus*** is the center and Lord of ***all*** creation, thus He should be the center and Lord of my life.

B. ***Jesus*** created me.

C. ***Jesus*** bought me.

D. ***Jesus*** rewards me with abundant life.

E. ***Jesus*** is the key to living a victorious, Spirit–filled Christian life.

F. ***Jesus*** can and will do a better job of running my life than I can, because ***He is:***

1. **God.**

2. **The powerful Controller of all things.**

3. **Faithful.**

STUDY

Notes

III. How can I allow Jesus Christ to be the center and Lord of my life?

A. ***Determine to just live one day at a time.*** Concentrate on allowing Jesus Christ to be the center and Lord of my life ***just for today.***

Reference: Matthew 6:9–13 (NKJV)

> In this manner, therefore, pray: Our Father in heaven, hallowed be Your name. Your kingdom come. Your will be done on earth as it is in heaven. Give us ***this day*** our daily bread. And forgive us our debts, as we forgive our debtors. And do not lead us into temptation, but deliver us from the evil one. For Yours is the kingdom and the power and the glory forever. Amen

B. ***Apply the formula*** God has given us for finding His ***direction*** and having our efforts crowned with ***success.***

STUDY

Reference: Proverbs 3:4–6 (LIV)

> If you want favor with both God and man, and a reputation for good judgment and common sense, then ***trust the Lord completely;*** don't ever trust yourself. ***In everything you do, put God first, and He will direct you and crown your efforts with success.***

Formula
Trust Christ completely
+
Put Christ first in everything you do
=
God-given direction and success

Notes

Let's pause here to discuss the importance of ***trusting Christ completely.***

1. **What does this mean?**
   It simply means to rely and depend upon Jesus without reservation, for more than just salvation.

2. **Why should I trust Christ completely?**

   a) Reference: Hebrews 11:6 (NKJV)

   > ***But without faith it is impossible to please Him,*** for he who comes to God must believe that He is, and that He is a rewarder of those who diligently seek Him.

   Answer . . .

   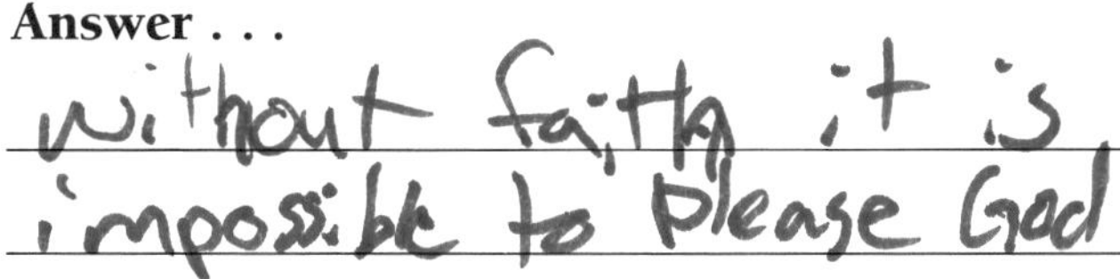

   b) Reference: Habakkuk 2:4

   > Behold, his soul which is lifted up is not upright in him: ***but the just shall live by his faith.***

   Reference: Romans 1:17 (NKJV)

   > For in it the righteousness of God is revealed from faith to faith: as it is written, ***"The just shall live by faith."***

   Reference: Galatians 3:11

   > But that no man is justified by the law in the sight of God, it is evident: for, ***The just shall live by faith.***

   Reference: Hebrews 10:38 (NKJV)

   > Now ***the just shall live by faith;*** but if anyone draws back, My soul shall have no pleasure in him.

STUDY

Notes

Answer . . .
The Just live by Faith

c) Reference: Proverbs 3:4–6 (LIV)

> If you want favor with both God and man, and a reputation for good judgment and common sense, then trust the Lord completely; don't ever trust yourself. In everything you do, put God first, and He will ***direct*** you and crown your efforts with ***success.***

Answer . . .
If we trust the Lord completely, God promises to give us direction and success.

d) Reference: Mark 9:23 (NKJV)

> Jesus said to him, "If you can believe, all things are possible to him who ***believes.***"

Reference: John 15:4–5 (NKJV)

> Abide in Me, and I in you. As the branch cannot bear fruit of itself, unless it abides in the vine, neither can you, unless you abide in Me. I am the vine, you are the branches. He who abides in Me, and I in him, bears much fruit; for without Me you can do ***nothing.***

STUDY

Answer . . .
All things are possible to him that believes.
But without Him we can do nothing.

e) Reference: Psalm 62:8 (NKJV)

> Trust in Him ***at all times,*** you people; pour out your heart before Him; God is a refuge for us.

Notes

Answer . . .
The Word instructs us to trust Him
at all times.

3. **How can I trust the Lord completely?**

a) ***Just for today*** don't depend on your own understanding, but rather ***depend on God*** for the following:

Reference: John 5:24 (NKJV)

> Most assuredly, I say to you, he who hears My Word and believes in Him who sent Me ***has everlasting life,*** and shall not come into judgment, but has passed from death into life.

Reference: John 10:28

> And I give unto them eternal life; and they ***shall never perish,*** neither shall any man pluck them out of my hand.

Answer . . .
S A L V a **T** i **O** n

Reference: 1 Corinthians 10:13 (JBP)

> No temptation has come your way that is too hard for flesh and blood to bear. But God can be trusted not to allow you to suffer any temptation beyond your powers of endurance. ***He will see to it that every temptation has a way out,*** so that it will never be impossible for you to bear it.

Answer . . .
D E L I V e **R** a **N C E**

STUDY

Notes

Reference: 2 Corinthians 12:9–10 (JBP)

His reply has been, "My grace is enough for you: for where there is weakness, my power is shown the more completely." Therefore, I have cheerfully made up my mind to be proud of my weaknesses, because they mean a deeper experience of the power of Christ. I can even enjoy weaknesses, suffering, privations, persecutions and difficulties for Christ's sake. For my very weakness makes me ***strong in Him.***

Answer . . .
S T R _ _ G T H

Reference: 1 Peter 5:5–7 (NKJV)

God resists the proud, but gives grace to the humble. Therefore humble yourselves under the mighty hand of God, that He may exalt you in due time, casting all your ***care*** upon Him, for ***He cares for you.***

Answer . . .
C O _ F O R T

Reference: Philippians 4:19 (NKJV)

And my God shall supply all your ***need*** according to His riches in glory by Christ Jesus.

Answer . . .
N _ _ D S

Reference: Proverbs 3:5–6 (NKJV)

Trust in the LORD with all your heart, and lean not on your own understanding; in all your ways acknowledge Him, and He shall **direct** your paths.

Answer . . .
D I R _ C T _ O N

STUDY

Notes

Reference: 1 John 1:9 (NKJV)

> If we confess our sins, He is faithful and just to ***forgive*** us our sins and to cleanse us from all unrighteousness.

Answer . . .
F O _ G _ V E N E S S

b) Let's assume that we see the importance of faith and have a desire for more faith. ***How do we increase or grow the faith God has given us?***

Reference: Luke 17:5–9 (NLT)

> One day the apostles said to the Lord, ***"We need more faith; tell us how to get it."*** "Even if you had faith as small as a mustard seed," the Lord answered, "you could say to this mulberry tree, 'May God uproot you and throw you into the sea,' and it would obey you! When a servant comes in from plowing or taking care of sheep, he doesn't just sit down and eat. He must ***first prepare his master's meal and serve him*** his supper before eating his own. And the servant is not even thanked, because he is merely doing what he is supposed to do."

Answer . . .
Always put God first.

Notice:

(1) The servant ***always puts the Master first.***

(2) This is part of the ***formula*** (on page 98), which tells us how to find ***God-given direction and success.***

STUDY

Notes

C. ***Make a total life commitment*** to allow Jesus Christ to be the center and Lord of your life. The evidence of this commitment is cultivating a lifestyle of denying self and yielding to God's control.

1. Total Life Commitment

Reference: Mark 8:34 (NKJV)

> When He had called the people to Himself, with His disciples also, He said to them, "Whoever desires to come after Me, let him ***deny himself*** and ***take up his cross,*** and ***follow Me.***"

Reference: Romans 6:13 (TCNT)

> Do not offer any part of your bodies to Sin, in the cause of unrighteousness but ***once for all offer yourselves to God*** (as those who, though once dead, now have life) and devote every part of your bodies to the cause of righteousness.

STUDY

2. Renew that Commitment Daily

Reference: Luke 9:23 (NKJV)

> Then He said to them all, If anyone desires to come after Me, let him deny himself, and take up his cross ***daily,*** and follow Me.

3. The ***result*** of this total commitment, renewed daily, denying self and yielding to God's control is the ***filling of the Holy Spirit,*** which simply means controlled by God.

   God's control in our lives is in direct proportion to the degree of our commitment, yielding and denial of self.

Notes

D. Realize the ***greatest hindrance*** to allowing Jesus Christ to be the center and Lord of your life is ***sin.*** When we sin, we grab back into our own hands the control we had yielded to God.

Now what do we do? We simply:

1. ***Confess*** the sin ***immediately.***

   Reference: 1 John 1:9 (NKJV)

   > If we ***confess*** our sins, He is ***faithful*** and just to ***forgive*** us our sins and to ***cleanse*** us from all unrighteousness.

2. Give ***(yield)*** the control ***back to God.***

   Reference: Romans 6:13

   > ***Yield yourselves unto God,*** as those that are alive from the dead, and your members as instruments of righteousness unto God.

   Reference: Joshua 24:23 (NIV)

   > ***Yield your heart to the LORD. . . .***

STUDY

Notes

Summary

How can I allow Jesus Christ to be the center and Lord of my life?

A. Determine to just ***live one day at a time.*** Concentrate on ***allowing Jesus Christ to be the center and Lord of your life just for today.***

B. Apply the ***formula*** God has given us for finding His ***direction,*** and having our efforts crowned with ***success.***

Formula
Trust Christ completely
+
Put Christ first in everything you do
=
God-given direction and success

C. Make a ***total life commitment to allow Jesus Christ to be the center and Lord of your life,*** and then ***renew that commitment daily.***

D. Realize that the ***greatest hindrance*** to allowing Jesus Christ to be the center and Lord of your life is ***sin.***

Learn to:

1. ***Confess*** sin immediately.

2. ***Yield*** the control back to God.

STUDY

Notes

STUDY

The spokes show ***the means by which Christ's power becomes operative in our lives.*** We maintain personal contact with God through the vertical spokes—the Word and prayer. ***The Word*** is our ***spiritual food*** as well as ***our sword*** for spiritual battle. It is the ***foundational spoke for effective Christian living.***

Notes

Saturating My Life with God's Word

I. What does this mean?

It simply means that by ***consistent daily intake of God's Word*** it somehow works itself, its words, its expressions, its teachings, its habits of thought and its presentation of the Father, Son and the Holy Spirit ***into every part of my being.***

II. Why saturate my life with God's Word?

Search the following scriptures for answers, and fill in the blanks.

A. Reference: Matthew 4:4 (NKJV)

> But He answered and said, It is written, Man shall not live by bread alone, ***but by every word*** that proceeds from the mouth of God.

I should saturate my life with God's Word because bread alone is not enough. God intends for us to feast on His **W**o r**D.**

B. Reference: Philippians 2:16 (NKJV)

> Holding fast ***the word of life,*** so that I may rejoice in the day of Christ that I have not run in vain neither labored in vain.

I should saturate my life with God's Word because it is the Word of **L** i **F** e.

C. Reference: Isaiah 55:11 (NKJV)

> So shall My word be that goes forth from My mouth; ***it shall not return to Me void, but it shall accomplish what I please,*** and it shall prosper in the thing for which I sent it.

STUDY

Notes

I should saturate my life with God's Word because it always accomplishes God's intended **P**u**RP**o**S**e.

D. Reference: 2 Timothy 3:16

> All scripture is given by ***inspiration*** of God, and is profitable for doctrine, for reproof, for correction, for instruction in righteousness.

Reference: 2 Peter 1:21 (NKJV)

> For prophecy never came by the will of man, ***but holy men of God spoke as they were moved by the Holy Spirit.***

I should saturate my life with God's Word because all scripture is given by **I**n**SP**I**R**A**T**I**O**N of God.

E. Reference: John 17:17 (NKJV)

> Sanctify them by Your truth. Your word is ***truth.***

I should saturate my life with God's Word because God's Word is **T**R**U**T**H.**

F. Reference: Hebrews 4:12 (RSV)

> For the Word of God is ***living and active,*** sharper than any two–edged sword, piercing to the division of soul and spirit, of joints and marrow, and discerning the thoughts and intentions of the heart.

I should saturate my life with God's Word because His Word is living and active.

G. Reference: Isaiah 40:8

> The grass withereth, the flower fadeth: but the word of our God shall stand ***forever.***

STUDY

Notes

I should saturate my life with God's Word because the Word of God will stand ________. It is enduring.

H. Reference: Psalm 19:7–11 (NIV)

> The law of the LORD is ***perfect,*** reviving the soul. The statutes of the LORD are ***trustworthy,*** making wise the simple. The precepts of the LORD are ***right,*** giving joy to the heart. The commands of the LORD are ***radiant,*** giving light to the eyes. The fear of the LORD is pure, enduring forever. The ordinances of the LORD are ***sure*** and altogether ***righteous.*** They are more ***precious*** than gold, than much pure gold; they are ***sweeter*** than honey, than honey from the comb. By them is your servant ***warned;*** in keeping them there is great ***reward.***

I should saturate my life with God's Word because His Word is: **P _ R F _ C T, T R U _ T W _ R T _ Y, R _ G _ T, R A D _ A N T, S _ _ E,** and **R I G _ T _ _ U S.** It is more **P R E _ I _ U S** than gold and **S W _ _ T E R** than honey and by it we are **W A _ N E D.** In obeying God's Word there is great **R E _ A _ D.**

STUDY

I. Reference: Psalm 107:20 (NKJV)

> He sent His word and ***healed*** them, and delivered them from their destructions.

I should saturate my life with God's Word because the Word of God **H _ A _ S.**

J. Reference: Psalm 119:130 (NKJV)

> The entrance of Your words gives ***light;*** it gives ***understanding*** to the simple.

Notes

I should saturate my life with God's Word because the Word of God gives **L __ G __ T** and **U __ D __ R __ T __ N __ I __ G.**

K. Reference: John 8:31–32 (AMP)

> So Jesus said to those Jews who had believed in Him, If you abide in My Word—hold fast to My teachings and live in accordance with them—you are truly My disciples. And you will know the ***truth,*** and the ***truth*** will set you ***free.***

I should saturate my life with God's Word because we have God's promise that if we ***stay in God's Word,*** and ***live in obedience*** to His teachings, we will know the **T __ U __ H,** and the __ **R** __ **T** __ will set us **F __ __ E.** The only real freedom in life is found in Jesus and His Word.

L. Reference: Romans 10:17 (NKJV)

> So then ***faith*** comes by hearing, and hearing by the word of God.

I should saturate my life with God's Word because the Word of God can produce **F __ I __ H.**

M. Reference: Psalm 119:162 (NLT)

> I ***rejoice*** in your Word, like one who finds a great treasure.

I should saturate my life with God's Word because God's Word gives me cause to rejoice. I can **R __ J __ I __ E** as one who has found a great treasure.

STUDY

Notes

N. Reference: Psalm 119:9–11 (LIV)

> ***How can a young man keep his way pure? By living according to your Word.*** I seek you with all my heart; do not let me stray from your commands. I have hidden your word in my heart ***that I might not sin against you.***

I should saturate my life with God's Word because God's Word holds me back from **S** I **N**.

O. Reference: Psalm 119:133 (NIV)

> ***Direct*** my footsteps according to your word; let no ***sin*** rule over me.

I should saturate my life with God's Word because then God **D I** R **E** C **T S** my footsteps so that no **S** I **N** can rule over me.

P. Reference: 1 Peter 1:23

> Being ***born again,*** not of corruptible seed, but of incorruptible, by the word of God, which liveth and abideth for ever.

I should saturate my life with God's Word because God's Word is the source of new **L** I **F** E.

Q. Reference: 1 Peter 2:2 (NKJV)

> As newborn babes, desire the pure milk of the word, that you may ***grow*** thereby . . .

Reference: Acts 20:32 (AMP)

> And now, brethren, I commit you to God—that is, I deposit you in His charge, entrusting you to His protection and care. And I commend you to the Word of His grace—to the commands and counsels and promises of His unmerited favor. ***It is able***

STUDY

Notes

to build you up and to give you [your rightful] inheritance among all God's set–apart ones—those consecrated, purified and transformed of soul.

I should saturate my life with God's Word because the Word of God is able to **BUILD** me up.

R. Reference: 2 Timothy 3:16

All scripture is given by inspiration of God, and is ***profitable for doctrine, for reproof, for correction, for instruction in righteousness.***

Diagram . . .

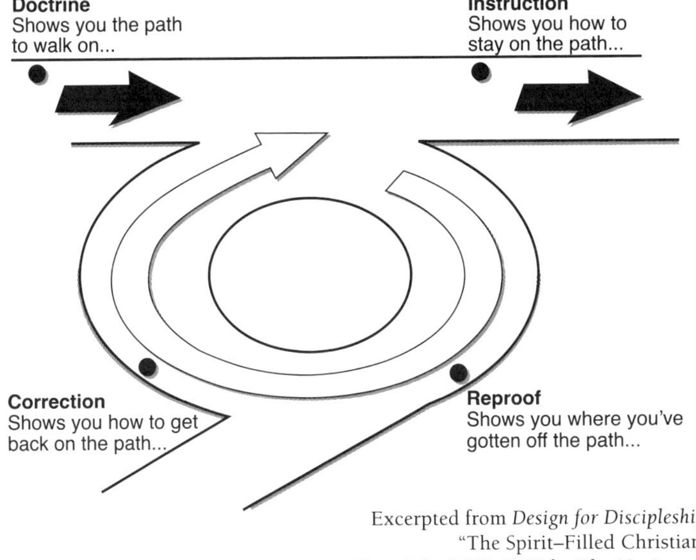

In light of the above scripture, God's Word is profitable for:

DOCTRINE

REPROOF

CORRECTION

INSTRUCTION

STUDY

Notes

In light of the above diagram, the purpose of:

Doctrine is to show us: ______________________________

____

Reproof is to show us: ______________________________

____

Correction is to show us: ____________________________

____

Instruction is to show us: ___________________________

____

S. Reference: Jeremiah 15:16 (NLT)

> Your words are what ***sustain*** me. They bring me great ***joy*** and are my heart's ***delight,*** for I bear your name, O Lord God Almighty.

I should saturate my life with God's Word because His words are what **S __ S __ A __ N** me. They bring me great **J __ Y** and are my heart's **D E __ I G __ T.**

T. Reference: 2 Timothy 3:17 (AMP)

> So that the man of God may be ***complete*** and ***proficient,*** well–fitted and thoroughly ***equipped*** for every good work.

I should saturate my life with God's Word because part of the intended purpose of God's Word is to help Christians to be **C __ M __ L __ T __** and **P __ O __ I __ I __ N __**, well–fitted and thoroughly **E __ U __ P P __ D** for every good work.

STUDY

Notes

U. God uses His Word in our lives in many ways. The way God uses His Word can be compared to:

1. Reference: Psalm 119:105 (NKJV)

Your word is a ***lamp*** to my feet and a light to my path.

L A M **P**

2. Reference: Jeremiah 23:29

Is not my word like as a ***fire?*** saith the LORD; and like a ***hammer*** that breaketh the rock in pieces?

F I **R** E and **H** A **M** M E **R**

3. Reference: Luke 8:11

Now the parable is this: The ***seed*** is the word of God.

S E **E** D

4. Reference: Ephesians 6:17

And take the helmet of salvation, and the ***sword*** of the Spirit, which is the word of God.

S W **O** R **D**

V. Reference: 1 John 5:13 (NKJV)

These things I have written to you who believe in the name of the Son of God, that you may know that you have ***eternal life,*** and that you may continue to believe in the name of the Son of God.

STUDY

Notes

I should saturate my life with God's Word because His Word assures us that we have **E _ E _ N _ L L _ F _.**

W. Reference: John 15:7 (NIV)

> If you remain in me and my words remain in you, ***ask*** whatever you wish, and it will be given you.

I should saturate my life with God's Word because God's Word aids **P R _ Y _ R.**

X. Reference: Joshua 1:8 (NLT)

> Study this Book of the Law continually. Meditate on it day and night so you may be sure to obey all that is written in it. Only then will you ***succeed.***

I should saturate my life with God's Word, meditate on God's Word and obey God's Word because only then will I **S U C _ E _ D.**

STUDY

Y. Reference: Psalm 119:1–3 (NLT)

> Happy are people of integrity, who ***follow*** the law of the Lord. Happy are those who ***obey*** His decrees and ***search*** for Him with all their hearts. They ***do not compromise*** with evil, and they ***walk*** only in His paths.

God gives true joy to those who **S E _ R _ H** for Him wholeheartedly and then **F O _ _ O W** and **O _ E Y** His Word without **C O _ P R _ M _ S E.**

Notes

Z. Reference: Proverbs 2:1–10 (LIV)

> Every young man who ***listens to Me and obeys*** My instructions will be given ***wisdom*** and ***good sense.*** Yes, if you want better ***insight*** and ***discernment,*** and are ***searching for them as you would for lost money or hidden treasure,*** then wisdom will be given you, and ***knowledge of God Himself;*** you will soon ***learn the importance of reverence for the Lord and of trusting Him.*** For the Lord grants wisdom! His every Word is a treasure of knowledge and ***understanding.*** He grants good sense to the godly—His saints. He is their ***shield, protecting*** them and ***guarding*** their pathway. ***He shows how to distinguish right from wrong, how to find the right decision every time.*** For wisdom and truth will enter the very center of your being, ***filling your life with joy.***

I should saturate my life with God's Word because of the promised results in the following ***formula*** taken from the above passage, Proverbs 2:1–10 (LIV):

Notes

Formula

Search the **W ___ R D** diligently

\+

Listen to God and **O B ___ Y**

=

A life blessed with the following

1. **W ___ S D ___ M.**
2. Good **S ___ N ___ E.**
3. **I N S ___ G ___ T.**
4. **D I S C ___ R ___ M ___ N T.**
5. **K N ___ W L ___ D ___ E** of **G ___ D** Himself.
6. Learning the importance of **R E V ___ R ___ N ___ E** for the **L O ___ D.**
7. Learning the importance of **T R ___ S T ___ N G** the **L O ___ D.**
8. **U N D ___ R ___ T ___ N D ___ N G.**
9. Being **S H ___ E ___ D ___ D** by **G ___ D.**
10. Being **P R ___ T ___ C T ___ D** by **G ___ D.**
11. Being **G ___ A ___ D ___ D** by God.
12. The ability to distinguish **R ___ G ___ T** from **W R ___ N G .**
13. The ability to find the **R ___ G ___ T D E C ___ S ___ O N** every time.
14. **J ___ Y .**

STUDY

Notes

Summary

Why saturate my life with God's Word?

You write the summary for this section. List ten reasons why a Christian should saturate his life with God's Word.

1. ____

2. ____

3. ____

4. ____

5. ____

6. ____

7. ____

8. ____

9. ____

10. ____

Notes

III. How can I saturate my life with God's Word?

A. **Ponder and Picture *what is involved.*** One of the best ways to do this is with the ***"hand" illustration,*** which shows us five methods of learning from the Bible. Each of these methods is important.

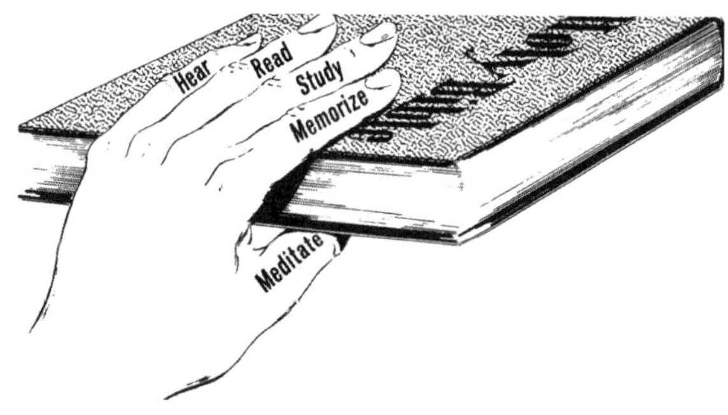

Copyright 1964 by The Navigators
Studies in Christian living.
"Walking with Christ"
Used by permission.

STUDY

1. Hear . . .

Hearing the Word from godly pastors and teachers provides us insight into others' study of the Scriptures as well as stimulating our own appetites for the Word.

a) Reference: Romans 10:17 (NKJV)

So then faith comes by hearing, and ***hearing*** by the word of God.

b) Reference: 1 Corinthians 1:21(NAS)

For since in the wisdom of God the world through its wisdom did not come to know God, God was well-pleased through the foolishness of the message ***preached*** to save those who believe.

Notes

c) Why do you think ***hearing*** God's Word preached and taught is important?

____

____

____

____

2. Read . . .

Reading God's Word daily ***allows the Word of God*** to flow over our lives ***to do its work of comforting*** in sorrow, ***guiding*** in perplexity, offering ***advice*** for our problems, ***rebuke*** for our sins and daily ***inspiration*** for our every need. Of course, ***the greatest purpose of the written Word of God, the Bible, is to reveal the living Word of God, the Lord Jesus Christ.***

STUDY

a) Reference: Revelation 1:3 (NKJV)

> Blessed is he who ***reads,*** and those who hear the words of this prophecy, and keep those things which are written in it; for the time is near.

b) Reference: Deuteronomy 17:19 (RSV)

> and it shall be with him, and he shall ***read*** in it all the days of his life, that he may learn to fear the Lord his God, by ***keeping*** all the words of this law and these statutes, and ***doing*** them.

c) Reference: 1 Timothy 4:13 (NKJV)

> Till I come, give attention to ***reading,*** to exhortation, to doctrine.

Notes

d) Questions concerning ***reading:***

(1) Do you think it would be a good idea for every Christian to read the entire Bible through every year of his life?
YES ❑ NO ❑

(2) If the average reader read the entire Bible through in a year, how long do you think it would take each day?

20 minutes ❑
45 minutes ❑
1 hour ❑
2 hours ❑

(3) What effect do you think reading through the Bible every year would have on the life of a Christian in twenty years?

____

____

____

____

STUDY

3. Study . . .

Studying the Scriptures ***leads us into personal discoveries of God's truths.*** Writing down these discoveries helps us organize and remember them better.

a) Reference: 2 Timothy 2:15 (AMP)

> ***Study*** and be eager and do your utmost to present yourself to God approved (tested by

trial), a workman who has no cause to be ashamed, ***correctly analyzing and accurately dividing—rightly handling and skillfully teaching—the Word of Truth.***

b) Reference: Acts 17:11

These were more noble than those in Thessalonica, in that they received the word with all readiness of mind, and ***searched the scriptures daily,*** whether those things were so.

c) One advantage of study is that we **W** __ **I** __ **E** down our discoveries of God's truths, and this helps us **O** __ **G** __ **N** __ **Z** __ and **R** __ **M** __ **M** __ **E** __ them better.

4. Memorize . . .

Memorizing God's Word ***enables us*** to use the sword of the Spirit to overcome Satan and temptations—to have it readily available for witnessing or helping others with a "word in season."

a) Reference: Proverbs 7:1–3 (NKJV)

My son, keep my words, and treasure my commandments within you. Keep my commands and live, and My law as the apple of your eye. Bind them on your fingers; ***write them on the tablet of your heart.***

b) Reference: Deuteronomy 6:6 (NKJV)

And these words which I command you today shall be ***in your heart.***

c) Reference: Psalm 119:11 (NIV)

I have ***hidden your word in my heart*** that I might not sin against you.

Notes

d) Why do you think a Christian should ***memorize*** God's Word?

____

____

____

5. Meditate . . .

Meditation is the thumb of the "hand" illustration, for it is ***used in conjunction with each of the other four methods. Only as we meditate on God's Word*—Ponder, Picture** and **Pray**—will we discover its ***transforming power*** at work in us. ***Meditation is the way we move truth from our head to our heart.***

a) Reference: Joshua 1:8 (NLT)

> Study this Book of the Law continually. ***Meditate on it day and night so you may be sure to obey all that is written in it.*** Only then will you ***succeed.***

b) Reference: Psalm 1:2 (NKJV)

> But his delight is in the law of the LORD, and in His law he ***meditates day and night.***

c) Reference: Psalm 119:97 (NKJV)

> Oh, how I love ***Your law! It is my meditation all the day.***

d) Why do you think a Christian should ***meditate*** on God's Word?

____

____

____

STUDY

Notes

B. ***Commit yourself*** to a ***lifetime project of mastering the Bible,*** and you will find that it is ***mastering you,*** and ***transforming*** your life by ***renewing*** your mind and heart.

1. Reference: Psalm 37:5 (LIV)

   Commit everything you do to the Lord. Trust him to help you do it and he will.

2. Reference: Romans 12:2 (JBP)

   Don't let the world around you squeeze you into its own mold, but ***let God remold your minds from within,*** so that you may prove in practice that the plan of God for you is good, meets all his demands and moves toward the goal of true maturity.

3. Why is a ***commitment*** to saturate my life with God's Word important?

   ____

   ____

   ____

STUDY

C. ***Discipline yourself*** to do the following:

   Regularly hear the Word of God preached and taught.

   Invest time alone with God each day—"Quiet Time." Try to meet with God for your "Quiet Time" at the same time and same place each day if possible. ***Talk with God*** through prayer, and ***allow Him time to talk to you*** through reading, studying, memorizing and meditating on His Word.

Notes

1. Reference: 1 Corinthians 9:24–27 (LIV)

   In a race, everyone runs but only one person gets first prize. So ***run your race to win. To win the contest you must deny yourselves many things that would keep you from doing your best.*** An athlete goes to all this trouble just to win a blue ribbon or a silver cup, but we do it for a heavenly reward that never disappears. ***So I run straight to the goal with purpose in every step. I fight to win. I'm not just shadow–boxing or playing around. Like an athlete I punish my body, treating it roughly, training it to do what it should, not what it wants to***. Otherwise I fear that after enlisting others for the race, I myself might be declared unfit and ordered to stand aside.

2. Reference: Romans 12:1 (AMP)

   I appeal to you therefore, brethren, and beg of you in view of [all] the mercies of God, to make ***a decisive dedication*** of your bodies—***presenting all your members and faculties—as a living sacrifice***, holy (devoted, consecrated) and well pleasing to God, ***which is your reasonable (rational, intelligent) service and spiritual worship.***

3. Is it likely that a Christian will saturate his life with God's Word without ***discipline?*** Why?

   ____

   ____

   ____

   ____

STUDY

Notes

D. ***Concentrate on just one day at a time.*** Don't worry about tomorrow. Just concentrate on getting some of the Word of God into your heart today.

1. Reference: Matthew 6:11

   Give us ***this day*** our daily bread.

2. Reference: Matthew 4:4

   But he answered and said, It is written, ***Man shall not live by bread alone, but by every word that proceedeth out of the mouth of God.***

3. Why be so concerned about getting some of the Word of God into your life ***today?***

   ____

   ____

   ____

   ____

   ____

   ____

   ____

   ____

Notes

Summary

How can I saturate my life with God's Word?

A. **Ponder and Picture** what is involved. The "hand" illustration:

1. ***Hear*** God's Word.
2. ***Read*** God's Word.
3. ***Study*** God's Word.
4. ***Memorize*** God's Word.
5. ***Meditate*** on God's Word.

B. ***Commit*** yourself to the ***lifetime project*** of allowing the Bible to master you.

C. ***Discipline*** yourself to:

1. ***Regularly hear*** the Word of God preached and taught.
2. Have a ***Quiet Time*** with God each day.

D. ***Concentrate*** on getting some of the ***Word of God*** into your heart ***today.***

STUDY

Notes

This is the spoke representing prayer. ***Through prayer*** we have ***direct communication*** with our heavenly Father and ***receive provision*** for our needs. As we pray we ***show our dependence*** upon and ***trust*** in Him.

STUDY

Notes

Saturating My Life with Prayer

I. What does this mean?

It simply means that ***conversation with God becomes a lifestyle,*** and not just an occasional thing. We ***cultivate natural loving responses to God throughout each day.*** These responses are ***expressed with words or thoughts of adoration, confession, thanksgiving or supplication,*** and the result is continuous fellowship with God.

II. Why saturate my life with prayer?

Search the following scriptures for answers, and fill in the blanks.

A. Reference: Proverbs 15:8

> The sacrifice of the wicked is an abomination to the LORD: but the prayer of the upright is his ***delight.***

I should saturate my life with prayer because the prayer of the upright is God's **D __ L __ G __ T.**

B. Reference: Jeremiah 33:3 (NKJV)

> Call to Me, and I will **answer** you, and show you ***great*** and ***mighty*** things, which you do not know.

I should saturate my life with prayer because the Lord says, "Call unto me, and I will **A __ S __ E R** you, and show you **G __ E __ T** and **M __ G H __ Y** things, which you do not know."

C. Reference: John 14:14 (NKJV)

> If you ask ***anything*** in My ***name,*** I will do it.

STUDY

Notes

I should saturate my life with prayer because Jesus said, "If you ask **A __ Y T __ I __ G** in My **N __ M __**, I will do it."

D. Reference: Philippians 4:6 (JBP)

> Don't worry over anything whatever; tell God every detail of your needs ***in earnest and thankful prayer.***

I should saturate my life with prayer because God's Word instructs me to let my requests be made known unto God by **P __ A __ E R.**

E. Reference: 1 Thessalonians 5:17–18

> Pray without ceasing. In every thing give thanks: for this is the ***will of God*** in Christ Jesus concerning you.

I should saturate my life with prayer because God's Word instructs me to pray without ceasing, and give thanks in everything, because this is the **W __ L __** of **G __ D.**

F. Reference: Hebrews 4:16

> Let us therefore come boldly unto the throne of grace, that we may obtain ***mercy,*** and find ***grace*** to help in time of need.

I should saturate my life with prayer because by prayer we obtain **M __ R __ Y** and find **G __ A __ E** to help in time of need.

G. Reference: Psalm 34:15, 17

> The eyes of the LORD are upon the righteous, and His ears are open unto their ***cry.*** . . . The righteous cry, and the LORD ***heareth,*** and ***delivereth*** them out of ***all*** their troubles.

STUDY

Notes

I should saturate my life with prayer because when I am in trouble, the ears of the Lord are open to the **C __ Y** of the righteous. The righteous cry, and the Lord **H __ A __ E __ H,** and **D __ L __ V __ R __ T __** them out of **A __ L** their troubles.

H. Reference: Matthew 7:7 (NKJV)

> ***Ask,*** and it will be given you; seek, and you will find; knock, and it will be opened to you.

I should saturate my life with prayer because Jesus instructed me to **A __ K.**

I. Reference: 1 John 1:9 (NKJV)

> If we ***confess our sins,*** He is faithful and just to forgive us our sins and to cleanse us from all unrighteousness.

STUDY

I should saturate my life with prayer because God's Word instructs me to **C __ N __ E __ S** my sins.

J. Reference: Ephesians 5:20 (RSV)

> Always and for everything giving ***thanks*** in the name of our Lord Jesus Christ to God the Father.

I should saturate my life with prayer because God expects me to pray, giving **T __ A __ K S** always and for everything.

K. Reference: 2 Chronicles 7:14

> If my people, which are called by my name, shall humble themselves, and pray, and seek my face, and turn from their wicked ways; then will I hear from heaven, and will forgive their sin, and will ***heal their land.***

Notes

I should saturate my life with prayer because prayer is essential if we are to experience **R E V __ V A L.**

L. Reference: Psalm 145:18 (RSV)

> The Lord is ***near*** to all who call upon him, to all who call upon him in ***truth.***

I should saturate my life with prayer because the Lord is **N __ A __** to all who call upon Him, to all who call upon Him in **T __ U __ H.**

M. Reference: James 5:16 (NKJV)

> Confess your trespasses to one another, and pray for one another, that you may be healed. The ***effectual, fervent*** prayer of a ***righteous*** man avails ***much.***

I should saturate my life with prayer because the **E __ F __ C __ U __ L, F __ R __ E __ T** prayer of a **R __ G __ T __ O __ S** man avails **M __ C __.**

Define the word ***fervent:***

____

____

____

____

N. Reference: Psalm 86:7 (NKJV)

> In the day of my trouble I will call upon You, for You will ***answer*** me.

I should saturate my life with prayer because in the day of trouble when I call upon God, He will **A __ S __ E R** me.

Notes

O. Reference: Matthew 26:41 (NKJV)

> Watch and pray, lest you enter into ***temptation.*** The spirit indeed is willing, but the flesh is weak.

I should saturate my life with prayer because prayer is an effective weapon in the face of **T __ M __ T __ T __ O __,** for it turns my attention to God at the very threshold of sin.

P. Reference: Matthew 21:22 (NKJV)

> And all things, ***whatever*** you ask in prayer, believing, you will ***receive.***

I should saturate my life with prayer because Jesus promised ***whatever*** you ask in prayer, believing, you will **R __ C __ I __ E.**

STUDY

Notes

Summary

Why saturate my life with prayer?

You write the summary for this section. List seven reasons why a Christian should saturate his life with prayer.

1. ____

2. ____

3. ____

4. ____

5. ____

6. ____

7. ____

Notes

III. How can I saturate my life with prayer?

A. **Ponder and Picture** ***what is involved:***

1. Some things that will assure me of having a more effective prayer life:

a) Reference: Matthew 6:7 (AMP)

> And when you pray ***do not (multiply words, repeating the same ones over and over,*** and) heap up phrases as the Gentiles do, for they think they will be heard for their ***much speaking.***

God does not hear us because we pray **L __ __ G** prayers. We are simply to let our requests be known unto God, believing that we will receive.

b) Reference: Luke 11:8–10 (AMP)

> I tell you, although he will not get up and supply him anything because he is his friend, yet because of his shameless ***persistence*** and ***insistence,*** he will get up and give him as much as he needs. So I say to you, ***Ask*** and keep on asking, and it shall be given you; ***seek*** and keep on seeking, and you shall find; ***knock*** and keep on knocking, and the door shall be opened to you. For every one who asks and keeps on asking receives, and he who seeks and keeps on seeking finds, and to him who knocks and keeps on knocking the door shall be opened.

Although God does not encourage long prayers just for long prayers' sake, He does encourage **P __ R __ I __ T __ N __ E** and **I __ S __ S __ E __ C __** for He says **A __ K** and keep on asking, **S __ __ K** and keep on seeking, **K __ O __ K** and keep on knocking.

STUDY

Notes

Define these words:

Persistence ______________________________

____

____

Insistence ______________________________

____

____

c) Reference: Matthew 6:5 (NIV)

> And when you pray, ***do not be like the hypocrites,*** for they love to pray standing in the synagogues and on the street corners to be seen by men. I tell you the truth, they have received their reward in full.

I should pray **S __ N __ E __ E __ Y.**

d) Reference: 1 Thessalonians 5:17

> ***Pray*** without ceasing.

I should go through each day fellowshipping with God in **P __ A __ E __** all through the day.

e) Reference: Hebrews 4:16

> Let us therefore come ***boldly*** unto the throne of grace, that we may obtain mercy, and find grace to help in time of need.

I should come **B __ L __ L __** to God in prayer.

STUDY

Notes

f) Reference: Mark 11:25 (NIV)

> And when you stand praying, if you hold anything against anyone, ***forgive*** him, so that your Father in heaven may forgive you your sins.

Before praying I should **F** __ **R** __ **I** __ **E** anyone I am holding a grudge against, so that God will forgive me.

g) Reference: Isaiah 59:2 (NKJV)

> But your iniquities have separated you from your God; And your ***sins*** have hidden His face from you, ***so that He will not hear.***

Your iniquities have separated you from your God; and your **S** __ **N** __ have hidden His face from you, so that He **W** __ **L** __ not hear.

Reference: 1 John 1:9

> If we ***confess*** our sins, he is ***faithful*** and just to ***forgive*** us our sins, and to ***cleanse*** us from ***all*** unrighteousness.

If we **C** __ **N** __ **E** __ **S** our sins, He is **F** __ **I** __ **H** __ **U** __ and just to **F** __ **R** __ **I** __ **E** us our sins, and to **C** __ **E** __ **N** __ **E** us from **A** __ __ unrighteousness.

Therefore, by confessing my sins I receive forgiveness and cleansing, and fellowship with God is restored because the sins that once separated me from God have been forgiven and forgotten.

STUDY

h) Reference: John 14:13 (NKJV)

> And ***whatever*** you ask ***in My name,*** that I will do, that the Father may be glorified in the Son.

And **W** __ **A** __ **E** __ **E** __ you ask **I** __ **M** __ **N** __ **M** __, that I will do, that the Father may be glorified in the Son. Therefore, I need to pray in the name of Jesus.

i) Reference: James 1:6–7

> But let him ask in **faith,** nothing wavering. For he that wavereth is like a wave of the sea driven with the wind and tossed. For let not that man think that he shall receive any thing of the Lord.

But let him ask in **F** __ **I** __ **H.** The man who doubts that he will receive what he asks, probably won't.

j) Reference: 1 John 5:14–15 (NKJV)

> Now this is the confidence that we have in Him, that ***if we ask anything according to His will,*** He hears us. And if we know that He hears us, ***whatever we ask, we know that we have the petitions that we have asked of Him.***

Always pray according to His **W I** __ __ .

Reference: Matthew 26:39 (NKJV)

> He went a little farther and fell on His face, and prayed, saying, "O My Father, if it is possible, let this cup pass from Me; ***nevertheless, not as I will, but as You will.***"

STUDY

Notes

Here we have the great example of our Lord, who prayed specifically, "O My Father, if it is possible, let this cup pass from Me." Then because of His great confidence in the Father, He was able to pray, "Nevetheless, not as I __ **I L L,** but as You **W __ L L.**" We demonstrate great confidence in God when we seek His will alone.

k) Reference: 1 John 3:22 (AMP)

> And we receive from Him whatever we ask for, because we (watchfully) ***obey*** His orders—observe His suggestions and injunctions, follow His plan for us—and (habitually) practice what is pleasing to Him.

O __ E __ I __ N __ E to what He has taught us is another key to receiving from Him whatever we ask.

STUDY

2. The following are examples of prayers from the Bible. Based on the information we discussed in the acrostic on page 82, check the box(es) that describe the following prayers.

a) Reference: Psalm 31:3 (NKJV)

> For You are my rock and my fortress; therefore, for Your name's sake, lead me and guide me.

A❑ C❑ T❑ S❑

b) Reference: John 17:20–24 (NKJV)

> I do not pray for these alone, but also for those who will believe in Me through their word; that they all may be one, as You, Father, are in Me, and I in You, that they also may be one in Us, that the world may believe that

Notes

You sent Me. And the glory which You gave Me I have given them, that they may be one just as We are one: I in them, and You in Me; that they may be made perfect in one, and that the world may know that You have sent Me and have loved them as You have loved Me. Father, I desire that they also whom You gave Me may be with Me where I am, that they may behold My glory which You have given Me; for You loved Me before the foundation of the world.

A❑ C❑ T❑ S❑

c) Reference: Psalm 139:23–24

Search me, O God, and know my heart: try me, and know my thoughts: And see if there be any wicked way in me, and lead me in the way everlasting.

A❑ C❑ T❑ S❑

d) Reference: Psalm 19:14 (NKJV)

Let the words of my mouth and the meditation of my heart be acceptable in Your sight, O LORD, my strength, and my Redeemer.

A❑ C❑ T❑ S❑

e) Reference: Psalm 36:5–11 (NKJV)

Your mercy, O LORD, is in the heavens; Your faithfulness reaches to the clouds. Your righteousness is like the great mountains; Your judgments are a great deep; O LORD, You preserve man and beast. How precious is Your lovingkindness, O God! Therefore the children of men put their trust under the shadow of Your wings. They are abundantly satisfied with

STUDY

Notes

the fullness of Your house, and You give them drink from the river of Your pleasures. For with You is the fountain of life; in Your light we see light. Oh, continue Your lovingkindness to those who know You, and Your righteousness to the upright in heart. Let not the foot of pride come against me, and let not the hand of the wicked drive me away.

A❑ C❑ T❑ S❑

f) Reference: Ephesians 3:14–21 (NKJV)

For this reason I bow my knees to the Father of our Lord Jesus Christ, from whom the whole family in heaven and earth is named, that He would grant you, according to the riches of His glory, to be strengthened with might by His Spirit in the inner man, that Christ may dwell in your hearts through faith; that you, being rooted and grounded in love, may be able to comprehend with all the saints what is the width and length and depth and height—to know the love of Christ which passes knowledge; that you may be filled with all the fullness of God. Now to Him who is able to do exceedingly abundantly above all that we ask or think, according to the power that works in us, to Him be glory in the church by Christ Jesus throughout all ages, world without end. Amen.

A❑ C❑ T❑ S❑

g) Reference: Psalm 51:1–2 (NKJV)

Have mercy upon me, O God, according to Your lovingkindness; according to the multitude of Your tender mercies, blot out my transgressions. Wash me thoroughly from my iniquity, and cleanse me from my sin.

Notes

All of Psalm 51 is a prayer, and the above two verses show us what kind of prayer it is.

A❑ C❑ T❑ S❑

h) Reference: Matthew 6:9–13 (NKJV)

> In this manner, therefore, pray: Our Father in heaven, Hallowed be Your name. Your kingdom come. Your will be done on earth as it is in heaven. Give us this day our daily bread. And forgive us our debts, as we forgive our debtors. And do not lead us into temptation, but deliver us from the evil one. For Yours is the kingdom and the power and the glory forever. Amen.

A❑ C❑ T❑ S❑

i) Reference: John 11:41 (NKJV)

> Then they took away the stone from the place where the dead man was lying. And Jesus lifted up His eyes and said, "Father, I thank You that You have heard Me."

A❑ C❑ T❑ S❑

STUDY

B. ***Commit yourself*** to a ***lifetime project of cultivating*** a close personal ***fellowship with God*** through ***prayer.***

Reference: Philippians 3:10 (AMP)

> ***[For my determined purpose is] that I may know Him—that I may progressively become more deeply and intimately acquainted with Him, perceiving and recognizing and understanding [the wonders of His Person] more strongly and more clearly.*** And that I may in that same way come to know the power outflowing from His resurrection [which it exerts over believers]; and that I

Notes

may so share His sufferings as to be continually transformed [in spirit into His likeness even] to His death, [in the hope]

Why is ***the commitment*** to saturate my life with prayer so important?

____

____

____

____

____

____

____

____

C. ***Discipline yourself*** to pray.

1. Have a "Quiet Time" with God each day, starting that day with prayer.

   Reference: Mark 1:35 (NKJV)

   > Now ***in the morning,*** having risen a long while ***before daylight,*** He went out and departed to ***a solitary place;*** and there ***He prayed.***

2. Cultivate natural loving responses of **A**doration, **C**onfession, **T**hanksgiving or **S**upplication to God all through each day.

   Reference: Ephesians 6:18 (NLT)

   > ***Pray at all times*** and on every occasion in the power of the Holy Spirit. Stay alert and be persistent in your prayers for all Christians everywhere.

STUDY

Reference: 1 Thessalonians 5:16–18 (RSV)

> ***Rejoice always, pray constantly, give thanks in all circumstances;*** for this is the will of God in Christ Jesus for you.

3. Define the word discipline.

____

____

____

4. Is it likely that a Christian will saturate his life with prayer without discipline? Why?

____

____

____

D. ***Concentrate on just one day at a time.*** Don't worry about tomorrow. Just concentrate on cultivating natural loving responses of **A**doration, **C**onfession, **T**hanksgiving and **S**upplication to God all through ***this day.***

1. Reference: Psalm 118:24 (NKJV)

> ***This is the day*** the LORD has made; we will rejoice and be glad in it.

2. Reference: Matthew 6:9–13 (NKJV)

> In this manner, therefore, pray: Our Father in heaven, Hallowed be Your name. Your kingdom come. Your will be done on earth as it is in heaven. Give us ***this day*** our daily bread. And forgive us our debts, as we forgive our debtors. And do not lead us into temptation, but deliver us from the evil one. For Yours is

Notes

the kingdom and the power and the glory forever. Amen.

3. Why be so concerned about cultivating those natural loving responses to God ***today?***

STUDY

Notes

Summary

How can I saturate my life with prayer?

A. **Ponder** and **Picture** what is involved.

B. ***Commit*** yourself to the lifetime project of cultivating a close personal fellowship with God through prayer.

C. ***Discipline*** yourself to pray:

1. Have a ***Quiet Time*** with God ***each day,*** starting that day with prayer.

2. ***Cultivate*** natural loving responses of **A**doration, **C**onfession, **T**hanksgiving and **S**upplication to God all through each day.

D. ***Concentrate*** on cultivating that close personal fellowship with God today. The greatest hindrance to cultivating this fellowship is the sin of procrastination.

Notes

STUDY

The obedient Christian in action is a loving person. You will find that this person:

1. ***Loves God*** wholeheartedly and devotedly.

2. ***Loves fellow Christians*** everywhere with a depth of love that distinguishes him from non–Christians.

3. ***Loves the lost,*** following the example of Jesus.

4. ***Loves and accepts himself*** with a strong, healthy, ***Christ–centered love.***

Notes

Saturating My Life with Love

I. What does this mean?

It simply means that ***by deliberate choice I allow the Holy Spirit to produce within me something that cannot be produced in its genuine form except by the Holy Spirit, and that is love.*** It is not an impulse from the emotions, nor does it always run with natural inclinations for it tenderly, unselfishly and kindly ***seeks the welfare of all,*** including the unlovely, and in fact, ***watches for opportunities to do good*** to all men. It is ***an attitude,*** but it can be ***recognized by the actions it prompts*** such as obedience to God, and serving fellow men.

II. Why saturate my life with love?

Search the following scriptures for answers, and fill in the blanks.

A. Why saturate my life with love for God?

1. Reference: John 3:16 (NIV)

   For God so loved the world that ***he gave his one and only Son,*** that whoever believes in him shall not perish but have eternal life.

   I should saturate my life with love for God because He loved me so much that He allowed **J __ S __ S** to die on the cross for my sins.

2. Reference: Romans 5:8 (RSV)

   But God shows his love for us in that while we were yet sinners ***Christ*** died for us.

   I should saturate my life with love for God because while we were yet sinners **C H __ I __ T** died for us.

S T U D Y

Notes

3. Reference: Psalm 31:23 (NLT)

    Love the LORD, all you faithful ones! For the LORD ***protects*** those who are loyal to Him, but harshly punishes all who are arrogant.

    I should saturate my life with love for God because the Lord **P R O __ E __ T S** those who are loyal to Him.

4. Reference: John 14:23 (AMP)

    Jesus answered, If a person [really] ***loves*** Me, he will keep My word—***obey*** My teaching; and My ***Father*** will love him, and We will come to him and make Our home (abode, special dwelling place) with him.

    I should saturate my life with love for God because Jesus promises that if we really **L __ V __** Him, we will **O __ E __** Him, and the **F __ T H __ R** will love us, and Jesus and the Father will come to live with us.

5. Reference: Psalm 145:20 (NKJV)

    The LORD ***preserves*** all who love Him, But all the wicked He will destroy.

    I should saturate my life with love for God because He **P R E __ E __ V __ S** all who love Him, but all the wicked He will destroy.

6. Reference: James 1:12 (NKJV)

    Blessed is the man who endures temptation; for when he has been approved, he ***will receive the crown of life*** which the Lord has promised to those who love Him.

STUDY

Notes

I should saturate my life with love for God because He has promised to **R E W __ R D** those that love Him and endure temptation.

7. Reference: 1 John 4:19

   We love him, because he first ***loved*** us.

   I should saturate my life with love for God because He first **L __ V __ D** me.

8. Reference: Ephesians 3:17 (AMP)

   May Christ through your faith [actually] dwell–settle down, abide, make His permanent home–in your hearts! May you be rooted deep in ***love*** and founded securely on ***love.***

   I should saturate my life with love for God because I am to be rooted deep in **L __ V __** and founded securely on **L __ V __.**

9. Reference: John 15:9–10 (AMP)

   I have loved you [just] as the Father has loved Me; abide in My love—continue in His ***love*** with Me. If you keep My commandments—if you continue to ***obey*** My instructions—you will abide in My love and live on in it; just as I have obeyed My Father's commandments and live on in His love.

   I should saturate my life with love for God because Jesus loves me deeply and has asked me to continue in His **L __ V __.** The way I continue to abide in His love is through
   O B __ D __ E __ C E to His teachings.

STUDY

Notes

10. Reference: Deuteronomy 10:12 (NKJV)

> And now, Israel, ***what does the Lord your God require of you,*** but ***to fear*** the Lord your God, ***to walk*** in all His ways and ***to love Him, to serve*** the Lord your God with all your heart, and with all your soul.

I should saturate my life with love for God because He requires that His people **L** __ **V** __ Him.

11. Reference: Deuteronomy 6:5 (NKJV)

> You shall ***love the Lord your God with all your heart,*** with all your soul, and with all your strength.

Reference: Deuteronomy 11:13 (NKJV)

> And it shall be that if you earnestly obey My commandments which I command you today, to ***love the Lord your God and serve Him with all your heart*** and with all your soul.

Reference: Joshua 22:5 (NIV)

> But be very careful to keep the commandment and the law that Moses the servant of the Lord gave you: ***to love the Lord your God,*** to walk in all his ways, to obey his commands, to hold fast to him and to serve him ***with all your heart*** and all your soul.

Reference: Matthew 22:37 (NKJV)

> Jesus said to him, ***"You shall love the Lord your God with all your heart,*** with all your soul, and with all your mind."

STUDY

Notes

Reference: Mark 12:30 (NKJV)

> And you shall ***love the Lord your God with all your heart,*** with all your soul, with all your mind, and with all your strength. This is the first commandment.

Reference: Luke 10:27 (NIV)

> He answered: "'***Love the Lord your God with all your heart*** and with all your soul and with all your strength and with all your mind'; and, 'Love your neighbor as yourself.'"

I should saturate my life with love for God because the Scripture teaches us to **L __ V E THE L__RD YOUR GOD W__TH ALL YO__ __ HE__RT.**

12. Reference: Joshua 23:10–11 (NKJV)

> One man of you shall chase a thousand, for the LORD your God is He who ***fights*** for you, as He promised you. Therefore take careful heed to yourselves, that you ***love the LORD your God.***

I should saturate my life with love for God because the Lord my God is the one that **F __ G H T __** for His people.

STUDY

Notes

Summary

Why saturate my life with love for God?

You write the summary for this section. List the three most important reasons why you think a Christian should saturate his life with love for God.

1. ______________________________

____

____

____

____

2. ______________________________

____

____

____

____

3. ______________________________

____

____

____

____

STUDY

Notes

B. Why saturate my life with love for fellow Christians?

1. Reference: Hebrews 13:1 (AMP)

   > Let love for your fellow believers continue and be a fixed practice with you—***never let it fail.***

   I should saturate my life with love for fellow Christians because this is to be a practice that never **F A __ L S.**

2. Reference: John 15:12–13 (NKJV)

   > This is My ***commandment,*** that you love one another, as I have loved you. Greater ***love*** has no one than this, than to lay down one's life for his friends.

   I should saturate my life with love for fellow Christians because this is Jesus' **C __ M M __ N D,** that we **L __ V __** one another as He loved us.

3. Reference: 1 John 4:7 (AMP)

   > Beloved, let us love one another; for love [springs] from God, and he who loves [his fellow men] is begotten (born) of God and is coming (progressively) to ***know*** and ***understand*** God—to perceive and recognize and get a better and clearer knowledge of Him.

   I should saturate my life with love for fellow Christians because it shows that I am coming to **K __ O __** and **U N __ E __ S T __ N D** God better.

4. Reference: 1 John 4:11

   > Beloved, if God so loved us, we ***ought*** also to love one another.

STUDY

Notes

I should saturate my life with love for fellow Christians because it is something I **O __ G __ T** to do since God loved me so much.

5. Reference: 1 Thessalonians 4:9 (NKJV)

> But concerning brotherly love you have no need that I should write to you, for you yourselves are ***taught by God*** to love one another.

I should saturate my life with love for fellow Christians. In fact, I should not have to be taught this lesson by someone, for this is **T __ U G __ T** by God.

6. Reference: 1 Peter 1:22 (AMP)

> Since by your obedience to the Truth through the [Holy] Spirit you have ***purified*** your hearts for the sincere affection of the brethren, [see that you] ***love one another fervently from a pure heart.***

I should saturate my life with love for fellow Christians because it is the proof of a
P __ R __ F I __ D heart.

7. Reference: 1 Peter 2:17 (LIV)

> Show respect for everyone. ***Love Christians everywhere.*** Fear God and honor the government.

I should saturate my life with love for fellow Christians because I am instructed to **L __ V __**
C __ R __ S __ I __ N S
E __ E __ Y W __ E __ E.

S T U D Y

Notes

8. Reference: 1 Peter 3:8 (NIV)

> Finally, all of you, live in ***harmony*** with one another; be sympathetic, **love** as brothers, be compassionate and humble.

I should saturate my life with love for fellow Christians because I am instructed to live in **H A R __ O N Y** with them and **L O __ E** them as brothers.

9. Reference: 1 John 3:23 (JBP)

> His ***orders*** are that we should put our trust in the name of His Son, Jesus Christ, and ***love one another—***as we used to hear Him say in person.

I should saturate my life with love for fellow Christians because God **O R D __ R S** me to love others.

10. Reference: 1 John 4:21 (AMP)

> And this command (charge, order, injunction) we have from Him, that he who loves God shall love his ***brother*** [believer] also.

I should saturate my life with love for fellow Christians because God's command is that those who love Him shall love their **B R __ T H __ R** also.

11. Reference: 1 Thessalonians 3:12 (NIV)

> May the Lord make your love ***increase*** and overflow for each other and for everyone else, just as ours does for you.

STUDY

Notes

I should saturate my life with love for fellow Christians, and that love should always be **I N C __ E __ S I N G.**

12. Reference: John 13:35 (JBP)

> ***This is how all men will know that you are my disciples,*** because you have such ***love*** for one another.

I should saturate my life with love for fellow Christians because that is how others will **K N __ W** that I am His disciple.

STUDY

Notes

Summary

Why saturate my life with love for fellow Christians?

You write the summary for this section. List the three most important reasons why you think a Christian should saturate his life with love for fellow Christians.

1. ____

____

____

____

____

2. ____

____

____

____

____

3. ____

____

____

____

____

STUDY

Notes

C. Why saturate my life with love for the lost?

1. Reference: 1 John 4:8 (NIV)

   Whoever does not love does not know God, because ***God is love.***

   I should saturate my life with love for the lost because if a person doesn't love others, it shows that he doesn't know God, for **G __ D** is **L __ V E**.

2. Reference: Ephesians 5:2 (LIV)

   Be full of ***love*** for others, following the example of ***Christ*** who loved you and gave Himself to God as a sacrifice to take away your ***sins.*** And God was pleased, for Christ's love for you was like sweet perfume to Him.

   I should saturate my life with love for the lost because I am to be full of **L __ V __** for others, following the example of **C H __ I __ T** who loved me and gave Himself to God as a sacrifice to take away my **S __ N __ .**

3. Reference: Leviticus 19:34 (NKJV)

   The ***stranger*** who dwells among you shall be to you as one born among you, and you shall love him as yourself; for you were strangers in the land of Egypt: I am the LORD your God.

   I should saturate my life with love for the lost because the Scripture instructs me to love the **S T R __ N __ E R.**

4. Reference: Matthew 19:19 (NKJV)

   'Honor your father and your mother,' and, 'You shall ***love your neighbor*** as yourself.'

STUDY

Notes

I should saturate my life with love for the lost because the Scripture instructs me to **L __ V __** my **N E __ G H __ O R.**

5. Reference: Matthew 22:39 (NKJV)

   And the second is like it: ***'You shall love your neighbor as yourself.'***

   I should saturate my life with love for the lost because the second greatest commandment is **Y O U S H __ L L L __ V __ Y O U R N E __ G H B __ R** as yourself.

6. Reference: Luke 6:27 (NKJV)

   But I say to you who hear: ***Love*** your ***enemies,*** do ***good*** to those who ***hate*** you.

   I should saturate my life with love for the lost because I am to **L __ V __** my **E N __ M __ E S** and to do **G __ O D** to those who **H __ T E** me.

7. Reference: Luke 6:35 (NKJV)

   But love your enemies, do good, and lend, hoping for nothing in return; and your ***reward*** will be great, and you will be sons of the Most High. For He is ***kind*** to the unthankful and evil.

   I should saturate my life with love for the lost because my **R E W __ R D** shall be great, and I will be responding like a true child of God, for He is **K __ N D** to the unthankful and wicked.

8. Reference: Matthew 5:44 (AMP)

   But I tell you, ***Love*** your ***enemies*** and ***pray*** for those who ***persecute*** you.

STUDY

Notes

I should saturate my life with love for the lost because the Scripture instructs me to **L __ V E** my **E N __ M __ E S** and **P R __ Y** for those who **P E R __ E __ U __ E** me.

9. Reference: Exodus 23:4 (NKJV)

   If you meet your enemy's ox or his donkey going astray, you shall surely ***bring it back*** to him again.

   I should saturate my life with love for the lost because the Scripture instructs me to inconvenience myself if necessary to **H E __ P** my enemy.

10. Reference: Proverbs 25:21 (NKJV)

   If your enemy is hungry, give him ***bread*** to eat; and if he is ***thirsty,*** give him water to drink.

   I should saturate my life with love for the lost because the Scripture instructs me to give my enemy **F O __ D** if he is hungry and water if he is **T H __ R S __ Y.**

11. Reference: Romans 12:19–21 (NIV)

   Do not take revenge, my friends, but leave room for God's wrath, for it is written: "It is mine to avenge; I will repay," says the Lord. On the contrary: "If your enemy is hungry, feed him; if he is thirsty, give him something to drink. In doing this, you will heap burning coals on his head." Do not be overcome by evil, but ***overcome evil with good.***

   I should saturate my life with love for the lost and take every opportunity to do good, even to my enemies, for maybe this will make them ashamed of themselves for what they have done.

STUDY

Notes

I am to conquer evil with **G O __ D** and leave the revenge to God.

12. Reference: Romans 13:9–10 (NIV)

> The commandments, "Do not commit adultery," "Do not murder," "Do not steal," "Do not covet," and whatever other commandment there may be, are summed up in this one rule: ***"Love your neighbor as yourself."*** Love does no harm to its neighbor. Therefore love is the ***fulfillment*** of the law.

I should saturate my life with love for the lost because love is the **F U L __ I L L M __N T** of the law.

13. Reference: Galatians 5:14 (NIV)

> The entire law is summed up in a single command: ***"Love your neighbor as yourself."***

I should saturate my life with love for the lost because the entire law is summed up in this one command: **L O __ E** your neighbor as yourself.

Notes

Summary

Why saturate my life with love for the lost?

You write the summary for this section. List the three most important reasons why you think a Christian should saturate his life with love for the lost.

1. ____________________

____

____

____

____

2. ____________________

____

____

____

____

3. ____________________

____

____

____

____

STUDY

Notes

III. How can I saturate my life with love?

A. How can I saturate my life with love for God?

1. I can saturate my life with love for God ***by cultivating an intimate, loving fellowship with God.***

a) I can ***cultivate*** an intimate, loving fellowship with God ***by investing quality time with Him*** and getting to know Him.

(1) Saturating my life with His Word.

(2) Saturating my life with prayer.

Reference: Philippians 3:10 (AMP)

> [For my ***determined purpose*** is] that I may ***know Him***—that I may progressively become more deeply and intimately ***acquainted*** with Him, perceiving and recognizing and understanding [the wonders of His Person] more strongly and more clearly. And that I may in that same way come to know the power outflowing from His resurrection [which it exerts over believers]; and that I may so share His sufferings as to be continually transformed [in spirit into His likeness even] to His death, [in the hope]

Paul said, "For my **D E T __ R M __ N __ D P U R __ O __ E** is that I may **K __ O __** Him—that I may progressively become more deeply and intimately **A C Q __ A __ N _ E D** with Him, perceiving and recognizing and understanding the wonders of His person more strongly and more clearly."

STUDY

Notes

b) I can ***cultivate*** an intimate, loving fellowship with God by ***learning to respond to God*** with natural loving responses of **A**doration, **C**onfession, **T**hanksgiving or **S**upplication all through each day.

(1) Reference: Ephesians 6:18 (NLT)

> ***Pray at all times*** and on every occasion in the power of the Holy Spirit. Stay alert and be persistent in your prayers for all Christians everywhere.

(2) Reference: 1 Thessalonians 5:16–18 (RSV)

> Rejoice always, ***pray constantly,*** give thanks in all circumstances; for this is the will of God in Christ Jesus for you.

(3) Learning to respond to God with natural loving responses of prayer all through each day will help me to cultivate an intimate, loving **F __ L L __ W S H __ P** with God.

c) I can ***cultivate*** an intimate, loving fellowship with God ***by yielding to the control of the Holy Spirit,*** for He is the one that produces the fruit of love.

(1) Reference: John 15:4 (NKJV)

> Abide in Me, and I in you. As ***the branch cannot bear fruit of itself,*** unless it abides in the vine, neither can you, unless you abide in Me.

(2) Reference: Philippians 2:13 (AMP)

> ***[Not in your own strength] for it is God Who is all the while effectually at work in***

STUDY

you—energizing and creating in you the ***power*** and ***desire***—both to will and to work for His good pleasure and satisfaction and delight.

(3) Reference: Galatians 5:22–25 (LIV)

But when the Holy Spirit controls our lives He will produce this kind of fruit in us: love, joy, peace, patience, kindness, goodness, faithfulness, gentleness and self–control; and here there is no conflict with Jewish laws. Those who belong to Christ have nailed their natural evil desires to his cross and crucified them there. ***If we are living now by the Holy Spirit's power, let us follow the Holy Spirit's leading in every part of our lives.***

(4) As I yield control of my life to the Holy Spirit, He is free to produce within me the fruit of **L __ V __ .** I simply bear the fruit as I abide in the vine. The Holy Spirit is the one that actually produces the fruit.

2. Pausing to ***evaluate*** the quality of my love for God can help me saturate my life with love for God.

a) Reference: 1 John 3:23–24 (AMP)

And this is His order (His command, His injunction), that we should ***believe—put our faith and trust in and adhere to and rely—on the name of His Son Jesus Christ, the Messiah,*** and that we should ***love one another,*** just as He has commanded us. All who ***keep His commandments*** (who ***obey*** His orders and follow His plan, live and continue to live, to stay and) abide in Him, and He in them.—They let Christ be a home to them and they

Notes

are the home of Christ. And by this we know and understand and have the proof that He [really] lives and makes His home in us, by the (Holy) Spirit Whom He has given us.

b) Reference: 1 John 2:4–5 (AMP)

Whoever says, I know Him—I perceive, recognize, understand and am acquainted with Him—but fails to keep and obey His commandments (teachings) is a liar, and the Truth [of the Gospel] is not in him. But he who keeps [treasures] His Word—who bears in mind His precepts, who observes His message in its entirety—truly in him has the love of and for God been perfected (completed, reached maturity). By this we may perceive and know and recognize and be sure that we are in Him:

c) The quality of my love for God can be evaluated by measuring three things in my life:

(1) The degree to which I believe—put my **F A __ T H** and **T R __ S T** in, and adhere to and rely—on **J __ S __ S.**

(2) The degree to which I **L __ V __** others.

(3) The degree to which I am **O B E __ I __ N T** to His commandments (teachings).

3. I can saturate my life with love for God by ***demonstrating*** my love for God.

Reference: John 14:15 (AMP)

If you [really] love Me you will ***keep (obey) My commands.***

STUDY

Notes

If I really love Jesus I will demonstrate that love by **O B __ Y __ N G** His commands (teachings).

4. I can saturate my life with love for God by ***con-centrating*** on loving God more ***today.***

Reference: Matthew 22:36–38 (NKJV)

> "Teacher, which is the great commandment in the law?" Jesus said to him, ***"You shall love the Lord your God with all your heart, with all your soul, and with all your mind."*** This is the first and great commandment.

When Jesus was asked, which is the greatest commandment, He replied, "You shall **L __ V__** the Lord your **G __ D** with all your heart, with all your soul, and with all your mind." Jesus was talking about loving Him more ***today,*** and not putting it off until tomorrow.

STUDY

Notes

Summary

How can I saturate my life with love for God?

1. **Cultivate** an intimate, loving fellowship with God by:

   a) ***Investing quality time with God*** and getting to know Him.

      (1) Saturating my life with His Word.

      (2) Saturating my life with prayer.

   b) Learning to ***respond to God with natural loving responses*** of **A**doration, **C**onfession, **T**hanksgiving or **S**upplication ***all through each day.***

   c) ***Yielding to the control of the Holy Spirit,*** for He is the one that produces the fruit of love.

2. **Evaluate** the quality of my love for God by measuring:

   - My faith in God.
   - My love for others.
   - My obedience to God.

3. **Demonstrate** my love for God by **obedience** to His teachings.

4. **Concentrate** on loving God more today.

STUDY

Notes

B. How can I saturate my life with love for others (fellow Christians and the lost)?

1. I can saturate my life with love for others (fellow Christians and the lost) ***by cultivating a love for them.***

   a) I can cultivate a love for others (fellow Christians and the lost) ***by seeing them as God sees them.***

   Reference: Ephesians 2:12 (NLT)

   > ***. . . living apart from Christ . . . excluded from God's people . . . without God and without hope.***

   Reference: John 10:10 (NKJV)

   > I have come that they may have ***life,*** and that they may have it more ***abundantly.***

   Jesus came that we may have **L I __ E.** Therefore, a person who has not received Christ into his/her life as his/her personal Savior and Lord is ***not really living, but just existing. He is lost and without hope.***

   And the ***Christian*** who is ***not trusting the Lord for everything*** has settled for life when he could have **A B __ N __ A N T** life.

   God saw our need and loved us enough to allow His only Son, Jesus, to die in our place that we might have abundant life.

   b) I can cultivate a love for others (fellow Christians and the lost) ***by learning how to respond to them.***

STUDY

Notes

Reference: Ephesians 4:31–32 (NLT)

> ***Get rid of all bitterness, rage, anger, harsh words, and slander, as well as all types of malicious behavior.*** Instead, be ***kind*** to each other, ***tenderhearted, forgiving*** one another, just as God through Christ has forgiven you.

I can cultivate a love for others (fellow Christians and the lost) ***by always responding to them by being:***

K __ N __
T __ N __ E __ H __ A __ T __ D
F __ R __ I __ I __ G

c) I can cultivate a love for others (fellow Christians and the lost) ***by yielding to the control of the Holy Spirit, for He is the one that produces the fruit of love.***

(1) Reference: John 15:4 (NKJV)

> Abide in Me, and I in you. As ***the branch cannot bear fruit of itself,*** unless it abides in the vine, neither can you unless you abide in Me.

(2) Reference: Philippians 2:13 (AMP)

> ***[Not in your own strength] for it is God Who is all the while effectually at work in you***—energizing and creating in you the power and desire—both to will and to work for His good pleasure and satisfaction and delight.

(3) Reference: Galatians 5:22–25 (LIV)

> ***But when the Holy Spirit controls our lives He will produce this kind of fruit***

STUDY

in us: love, joy, peace, patience, kindness, goodness, faithfulness, gentleness and self–control; and here there is no conflict with Jewish laws. Those who belong to Christ have nailed their natural evil desires to his cross and crucified them there. ***If we are living now by the Holy Spirit's power, let us follow the Holy Spirit's leading in every part of our lives.***

(4) When the **H __ LY SP __ RIT** controls my life, ***He will produce in me a*** **L __ V __** ***for others.***

2. I can saturate my life with love for others (fellow Christians and the lost) ***by pausing to evaluate the quality of my love for them. I can evaluate the quality of my love for others by giving myself the following test:***

a) Reference: 1 Corinthians 13:4 (NLT)

Love is ***patient*** and kind. Love is not jealous or boastful or proud.

Reference: 1 Thessalonians 5:14 (LIV)

Dear brothers, warn those who are lazy; comfort those who are frightened; take tender care of those who are weak; and **be patient with everyone.**

Am I **P __ T __ E __ T** with everyone?

b) Reference: 1 Corinthians 13:4 (NLT)

Love is patient and ***kind.*** Love is not jealous or boastful or proud.

Notes

Reference: 2 Timothy 2:24 (RSV)

> And the Lord's servant must not be quarrelsome but ***kindly to every one,*** an apt teacher, forbearing . . .

Am I **K __ N D** to everyone?

c) Reference: 1 Corinthians 13:4 (NLT)

> Love is patient and kind. Love is not ***jealous*** or boastful or proud.

Reference: 1 Peter 2:1 (AMP)

> So be done with every trace of wickedness (depravity, malignity) and all deceit and insincerity (pretense, hypocrisy) and grudges ***(envy, jealousy)*** and slander and evil speaking of every kind.

Am I ever **E __ V I __ U S** or **J __ A __ O __ S** of anyone?

d) Reference: 1 Corinthians 13:4 (NLT)

> Love is patient and kind. Love is not jealous or ***boastful or proud.***

Reference: Proverbs 16:5 (LIV)

> ***Pride disgusts the Lord.*** Take my word for it—***proud men shall be punished.***

Am I ever **P __ O __ D** or **B __ A __ T __ U L** around others?

e) Reference: 1 Corinthians 13:5 (NKJV)

> does not behave ***rudely,*** does not seek its own, is not provoked, thinks no evil.

STUDY

Reference: Romans 13:10 (LIV)

> ***Love does no wrong to anyone.*** That's why it fully satisfies all of God's requirements. It is the only law you need.

Do I ever wrong others by being **R __ D __** to them?

f) Reference: 1 Corinthians 13:5 (NKJV)

> does not behave rudely, ***does not seek its own,*** is not provoked, thinks no evil.

Reference: 1 Corinthians 10:24 (LIV)

> ***Don't think only of yourself.*** Try to think of the other fellow, too, and what is best for him.

Am I ever **S E __ F __ S H** around others, demanding my own way?

g) Reference: 1 Corinthians 13:5 (NLT)

> . . . Love does not demand its own way. Love is not ***irritable,*** and it ***keeps no record of when it has been wronged.***

Reference: Proverbs 10:12 (LIV)

> Hatred stirs old quarrels, but ***love overlooks insults.***

Am I ever **I __ R __ T __ B L E** or **U N __ O R __ I __ I N G** toward others?

h) Reference: 1 Corinthians 13:6 (NEB)

> ***does not gloat over other men's sins,*** but delights in the truth.

STUDY

Notes

Reference: Proverbs 24:17 (LIV)

> ***Do not rejoice when your enemy meets trouble.*** Let there be no gladness when he ***falls*** . . .

Do I rejoice when others **S __ N** or **F __ L L?**

i) Reference: 1 Corinthians 13:6 (NEB)

> . . . does not gloat over other men's sins, but **delights in the truth.**

Reference: 2 John 4 (AMP)

> I was greatly delighted to find some of your children walking (living) in [the] ***Truth,*** just as we have been commanded by the Father [Himself].

Am I delighted when I see others walking (living) in the **T R __ T H ?**

j) Reference: 1 Corinthians 13:7

> ***Beareth all things,*** believeth all things, hopeth all things, endureth all things.

Reference: Galatians 6:2 (NKJV)

> ***Bear one another's burdens,*** and so fulfill the law of Christ.

Do I help others by bearing their **B __ R D __ N S (carry them to Jesus and leave them there)?**

k) Reference: 1 Corinthians 13:7 (LIV)

> If you love someone you will be ***loyal*** to him no matter what the cost. You will always believe in him, always expect the best of him, and always stand your ground in defending him.

STUDY

Notes

Reference: Luke 6:36–37 (NIV)

Be merciful, just as your Father is merciful. Do not judge, and you will not be judged. Do not ***condemn,*** and you will not be condemned. Forgive, and you will be forgiven.

Am I **L _ Y _ L** to others or do I **C _ N _ E M N** them?

l) Reference: 1 Corinthians 13:7 (NKJV)

bears all things, believes all things, ***hopes all things,*** endures all things.

Reference: 2 Corinthians 1:7 (AMP)

And our hope for you—that is, our joyful and confident expectation of good for you—is ever unwavering, (assured and unshaken); for we know that just as you share and are partners in [our] sufferings and calamities, you also share and are partners in [our] comfort (consolation and encouragement).

Do I **H __ P __** for the best in the lives of others?

m) Reference: 1 Corinthians 13:7 (NKJV)

bears all things, believes all things, hopes all things, ***endures all things.***

Reference: Galatians 6:9–10 (LIV)

And let us not get tired of doing what is right, for after a while we will reap a harvest of blessing if we ***don't get discouraged and give up.*** That's why whenever we can we should always be kind to everyone, and especially to our Christian brothers.

S
T
U
D
Y

Notes

Is my love **E N D __ R __ N G,** or do I get discouraged and give up when attempting to love others?

n) Reference: 1 Corinthians 13:8 (NLT)

> ***Love will last forever,*** but prophecy and speaking in unknown languages and special knowledge will all disappear.

Reference: 1 Thessalonians 3:12 (NLT)

> ***And may the Lord make your love grow and overflow to each other and to everyone else,*** just as our love overflows toward you.

Is my love for fellow Christians and the lost **G R __ W __ N G** and **O V __ R F L __ W __ N G?**

STUDY

Notes

3. I can saturate my life with love for others (fellow Christians and the lost) ***by demonstrating my love for them.***

   a) I can ***demonstrate*** my love for others (fellow Christians and the lost) ***by applying the principles I just studied*** while evaluating the quality of my love for others.

      (1) Be **P A T __ E N T.**

      (2) Be **K __ N D.**

      (3) Don't be **J E__ L O__ S.**

      (4) Don't be **P R __ U D** or **B O __ S T __ U L.**

      (5) Don't be **R __ D E.**

      (6) Don't be **S E L __ __ S H.**

      (7) Don't be **I R R __ T A __ L E** or **U N F __ R G I __ I N G.**

      (8) Don't rejoice when others **S __ N** or **F __ L L.**

      (9) Be delighted when you see others walking (living) in the **T R __ T H.**

      (10) Help bear the **B U __ D E __ S** of others.

      (11) Don't be **C O N __ E M N I N G,** but be **L O __ A L** and believe the best about others.

      (12) **H __ P E** for the best in the lives of others.

STUDY

Notes

(13) **E N __ U R E,** don't get discouraged and give up.

(14) Keep your love **G R __ W I __ G** and **O V E __ F L __ W I N G.**

b) I can demonstrate my love more specifically for fellow Christians through fellowship.

The ***fellowship*** we are called to is one of:

(1) Reference: Psalm 133:1–3 (LIV)

> How wonderful it is, how pleasant, when brothers live in ***harmony!*** For ***harmony*** is as precious as the fragrant anointing oil that was poured over Aaron's head, and ran down onto his beard, and onto the border of his robe. ***Harmony*** is as refreshing as the dew on Mount Hermon, on the mountains of Israel. And God has pronounced this eternal blessing on Jerusalem, even life forevermore.

Reference: Philippians 1:27 (AMP)

> Only be sure as citizens so to conduct yourselves that your manner of life will be worthy of the good news (the Gospel) of Christ, so that whether I [do] come and see you or am absent, I may hear this of you: that you are ***standing firm in united spirit and purpose, striving side by side and contending with a single mind*** for the faith of the glad tidings (the Gospel).

H A R __ O __ Y

STUDY

Notes

(2) Reference: 1 John 1:3 (AMP)

> What we have seen and [ourselves] heard we are also telling you, so that you too may realize and enjoy fellowship as ***partners*** and partakers with us. And [this] fellowship that we have (which is a distinguishing mark of Christians) is with the Father and with His Son Jesus Christ, the Messiah.

Reference: Colossians 2:2 (NLT)

> My goal is that they will be encouraged and ***knit together by strong ties of love.*** I want them to have full confidence because they have complete understanding of God's secret plan, which is Christ Himself.

P A R __ N __ R S H I P

(3) Reference: Philippians 4:14–15 (RSV)

> Yet it was kind of you to ***share*** my trouble. And you Philippians yourselves know that in the beginning of the gospel, when I left Macedonia, no church entered into partnership with me in giving and receiving except you only.

Reference: 2 Corinthians 8:1–5 (JBP)

> Now, my brothers, we must tell you about the grace that God has given to the Macedonian churches. Somehow, in most difficult circumstances, their joy and the fact of being down to their last penny themselves, produced a magnificent concern for other people. I can guarantee that ***they were willing***

STUDY

Notes

to give to the limit of their means, yes and beyond their means, without the slightest urging from me or anyone else. ***In fact they simply begged us to accept their gifts*** and so let them ***share*** the honor of supporting their brothers in Christ. ***Nor was their gift,*** as I must confess I had expected, ***a mere cash payment.*** Instead they made a complete dedication of themselves first to the Lord and then to us, as God's appointed ministers.

S H A __ I N G

(4) Reference: Acts 2:42 (LIV)

They joined with the other believers in regular attendance at the apostles' teaching sessions and at the Communion services and prayer meetings.

Reference: Hebrews 10:24–25 (AMP)

And let us consider and give attentive, continuous care to watching over one another, studying how we may stir up (stimulate and incite) to love and helpful deeds and noble activities; ***Not forsaking or neglecting to assemble together*** [as believers], as is the habit of some people, but admonishing—warning, urging and encouraging—one another, and all the more faithfully as you see the day approaching.

T O G __ T H E __ N E S S

STUDY

Notes

c) I can demonstrate my love more specifically for the lost through witnessing.

(1) Reference: Colossians 1:28–29 (LIV)

> ***So everywhere we go we talk about Christ to all who will listen,*** warning them and teaching them as well as we know how. We want to be able to present each one to God, perfect because of what Christ has done for each of them. This is my work, and I can do it only because Christ's mighty energy is at work within me.

I demonstrate my love for the lost by talking about **C H R __ S T** everywhere I go.

(2) Reference: Matthew 28:18–20 (NIV)

> Then Jesus came to them and said, "All authority in heaven and on earth has been given to me. Therefore go and make ***disciples*** of all nations, baptizing them in the name of the Father and of the Son and of the Holy Spirit, and teaching them to obey everything I have commanded you. And surely I am with you always, to the very end of the age."

I demonstrate my love for the lost when I go and make **D __ S C I __ L E S.**

(3) Reference: Matthew 4:19 (NLT)

> Jesus called out to them, "Come, be my disciples, and I will show you how to fish for ***people!***"

STUDY

Notes

I demonstrate my love for the lost by learning to fish for **P E __ P __ E.**

(4) Reference: Romans 1:16 (AMP)

> For I am ***not ashamed*** of the Gospel (good news) of Christ; for it is God's power working unto salvation (for deliverance from eternal death) to every one who believes with a personal trust and a confident surrender and firm reliance, to the Jew first and also to the Greek.

I demonstrate my love for the lost by witnessing, and I witness for I am not **A S H __ M __ D** of the Gospel of Christ.

(5) Reference: 1 Peter 3:15 (NEB)

> Hold the Lord Christ in reverence in your hearts. Be always ready with your defense whenever you are called to account for the ***hope*** that is in you, but make that defense with ***modesty*** and ***respect.***

I demonstrate my love for the lost by always being ready to give an account for the **H __ P E** that is in me with modesty and **R E S __ E __ T.**

(6) Reference: Proverbs 11:30 (NIV)

> The fruit of the righteous is a tree of life, and he who wins souls is ***wise.***

It is an act of love to witness to the lost, but it is also **W __ S __ .**

STUDY

Notes

4. I can saturate my life with love for others (fellow Christians and the lost) ***by concentrating on loving them more today.***

   Reference: Matthew 22:39 (NIV)

   > And the second is like it: '***Love*** your neighbor as yourself.'

   The second greatest commandment is to **L** __ **V** __ others as much as you love yourself.

   The only way it is possible to love others as much as we love ourselves is to ***yield*** to the Holy Spirit and ***concentrate*** on just a few principles each day. Finally, the Holy Spirit will begin to strengthen our weaknesses and give us victory, little by little, as He transforms us into a more loving person.

Notes

Summary

How can I saturate my life with love for others (fellow Christians and the lost)?

1. ***Cultivate*** a love for others by:

   a) ***Seeing them as God sees them.***

   b) Learning to ***respond to them*** by being:

      - **Kind.**
      - **Tenderhearted.**
      - **Forgiving.**

   c) ***Yielding to the control of the Holy Spirit,*** for He is the one that produces the fruit of love.

2. ***Evaluate*** the quality of my love for others by giving myself the ***love test.***

3. ***Demonstrate*** my love for others by ***applying the principles*** taught in the love test. In addition to applying these principles I can demonstrate my love for:

   - Fellow Christians through ***fellowship.***
   - The lost through ***witnessing.***

4. ***Concentrate*** on loving others more today by:

   - ***Yielding to the control of the Holy Spirit,*** for He produces the fruit of love.

   - ***Concentrate on improving*** the quality of my love in one specific area each day. For example, ***today*** work on patience, or kindness or unselfishness.

STUDY

Notes

C. How can I saturate my life with love for God and others?

I can saturate my life with love for God and others ***by having a Christ–centered love for myself and accepting myself just as I am.***

Reference: Romans 12:3 (NEB)

> In virtue of the gift that God in His grace has given me I say to everyone among you: ***do not be conceited or think too highly of yourself;*** but think your way to a sober estimate based on the measure of faith that God has dealt to each of you.

Reference: Matthew 22:39 (LIV)

> The second most important is similar: Love your neighbor as much as you love ***yourself.***

Though I am not to be **C O N __ E __ T E D** or think too **H I G _ L Y** of myself, yet I am to love others as much as I love **M Y __ E __ F**, and that implies that I should have a strong, healthy, Christ–centered love for myself.

To realize the following will help me to have a healthy, Christ–centered love for myself:

1. Reference: Philippians 2:13 (AMP)

   > ***[Not in your own strength]*** for it is God Who is all the while effectually at work in you—energizing and creating in you the power and desire—both to will and to work for His good pleasure and satisfaction and delight.

   To realize how dependent I am on Jesus will keep me from thinking more highly of myself than I should. My highest potential is out of

STUDY

Notes

reach unless I ***yield to the control of the Holy Spirit,*** and ***abide in Jesus,*** for ***He transforms*** my weaknesses into strengths, and ***He produces*** the fruit in my life, and this is not done in my own **S T __ E N __ T H.**

2. Reference: Psalm 139:13–15 (LIV)

   You made ***all*** the ***delicate,*** inner parts of my body, and knit them together in my mother's womb. Thank you for making me so wonderfully complex! It is amazing to think about. Your workmanship is marvelous—and how well I know it. You were there while I was being formed in utter seclusion!

   God designed and created me. He made **A __ L** the **D __ L __ C __ T E,** inner parts of my body and knit them together in my mother's womb. Should I reject, hate or complain about something God has designed and created?

STUDY

3. Reference: Jeremiah 29:11 (LIV)

   For I know the ***plans*** I have for you, says the Lord. They are ***plans*** for ***good*** and not for evil, to give you a ***future*** and a ***hope.***

   Reference: Psalm 139:16 (LIV)

   You saw me before I was born and ***scheduled each day of my life before I began to breathe.*** Every day was recorded in your Book!

   God designed and created me for a purpose. God has plans for my life, and they are **P __ A __ S** for **G __ __ D** and not for evil, to give me a **F __ T __ R E** and a **H __ P E.**

Notes

4. Reference: Psalm 139:1–12,17–18 (NLT)

 O LORD, you have examined my heart and know ***everything*** about me. You know when I sit down or stand up. You know my every thought when far away. You chart the ***path*** ahead of me and tell me where to stop and rest. Every ***moment*** you know where I am. You know what I am going to say even ***before*** I say it, LORD. You both ***precede*** and ***follow*** me. You place your hand of blessing on my head. Such knowledge is too wonderful for me, too great for me to know! I can never escape from your Spirit! ***I can never get away from your presence!*** If I go up to heaven, you are there; if I go down to the place of the dead, you are there. If I ride the wings of the morning, If I dwell by the farthest oceans, even there your hand will ***guide*** me, and your ***strength*** will support me. I could ask the darkness to hide me and the light around me to become night—but ***even in darkness I cannot hide from you.*** How precious are ***your thoughts about me,*** O God! They ***are innumerable!*** I can't even count them; they outnumber the grains of sand! ***And when I wake up in the morning, you are still with me!***

At this moment God loves me and is very interested in me personally. He is concerned about every detail of my life.

He knows **E __ E R Y __ H __ N G** about me.

He charts the **P __ T H** ahead of me.

Every **M __ M __ N T** He knows where I am.

He knows what I am going to say **B __ F O __ E** I even say it.

STUDY

Notes

He both **PRE __ E __ ES** and **F __ LL __ WS** me.

I can never get away from **G __ D.**

His hand **G __ I __ ES** me and his **ST __ EN __ TH** supports me.

Even in darkness I cannot **H __ DE** from God.

The Lord is thinking about me **CON __ IN __ A __ LY.**

The Lord is always **W __ TH** me.

STUDY

Notes

Summary

How can I saturate my life with love for God and others?

If I am to love God and others as much as I should, then I must have a strong, healthy, ***Christ–centered love for myself*** and ***accept myself just as I am.*** On the other hand, ***I am not to be prideful and think more highly of myself than I should.***

I need to develop a strong, healthy, Christ–centered love for myself without becoming prideful, and I can do this by realizing:

1. How ***dependent*** I am ***on Jesus.***

2. That ***God designed*** and ***created me.***

3. That God designed and created me for a ***purpose.***

4. That ***God loves me*** and is very ***interested in me personally.*** He is interested in every detail of my life.

STUDY

Notes

Daily Bible Study Challenge

After Session 15:

1. ***Search out some method*** or methods of personal daily Bible Study that are meaningful and helpful to you (consider the ***"Helps in Personal Bible Study"*** on the following page).

2. ***Be diligent and disciplined*** in applying yourself to personal daily Bible Study.

3. ***Set some goals*** in personal daily Bible Study, and work toward them with a great deal of determination.

4. ***Obey and apply*** that which God teaches you through personal daily Bible Study.

STUDY

Notes

Helps in Personal Bible Study

There are many valuable methods of Bible Study. One may study the Bible, as it were, with a ***telescope***, to see the great truths that stand out in every book. Or one may study the Bible with a ***microscope*** to find all of the marvelous details that are in this mine of spiritual riches. ***In the next few pages you will find the following seven proven methods for a more intensive, personal Bible Study:***

1. Bible Study by **Chapters**
2. Bible Study by **Paragraphs**
3. Bible Study by **Verses**
4. Bible Study by **Books**
5. Bible Study by **Words**
6. Bible Study by **Topics**
7. Bible Study by **Biography**

Remember, ***Bible Study is one way of saturating your life with God's Word and learning more about Jesus and the lifestyle He teaches.***

The great thrill of Bible Study is ***discovering*** the eternal truths of God's Word for yourself and embarking on the adventure of ***obeying*** them and ***experiencing the blessing*** in your personal life.

The "Help in Personal Bible Study" and "Methods of Bible Study" were excerpted and/or paraphrased from the *New Encyclopedic Reference Edition* of the Bible.

STUDY

Notes

Methods of Bible Study

I. Bible Study by Chapters

In the Bible there are 1,189 chapters in the Old and New Testaments. In a little over three years a person could make an intensive study of the whole Bible, just taking a chapter a day. It is usually a good practice to start your Bible Study in the New Testament.

A. ***Read*** the chapter carefully to find the main subject or subjects. You may find it necessary to read the preceding and following chapters.

B. Give the chapter a ***title*** that suggests its main content.

C. ***Reread*** and ***make*** a simple ***outline*** of the chapter.

D. ***Ask and answer*** the following questions concerning each chapter:

1. What is the main ***subject*** or subjects of this chapter?
2. Who are the ***persons*** revealed in this chapter? Who is speaking? About whom is he speaking?
3. What is the ***key verse*** of this chapter?
4. What does this chapter ***teach*** me about the Lord Jesus Christ?
5. Is there any ***sin*** for me to confess and forsake mentioned in this chapter?
6. Is there any ***command*** for me to obey in this chapter?
7. Is there any ***promise*** for me to claim in this chapter?

STUDY

8. Is there any ***instruction*** for me to follow in this chapter?
9. Is there any ***prayer*** that I should pray in this chapter?

E. ***List and define*** the ***key words*** in this chapter.

F. Since it is important to compare scripture to scripture to find its true meaning, ***find and read*** other portions of the Bible that discuss the main subject of this chapter.

G. ***List the truths*** God has revealed to me through this study that I should apply to my life.

H. **Ponder — *seriously think*** about these truths. What is God saying to me personally?

I. **Picture — *form a mental picture*** of these truths. ***See*** myself in the ***picture*** and ***imagine*** my response.

J. **Pray — *talk to God*** about applying these truths. Pray these truths back to God as my personal prayer of **A**doration, **C**onfession, **T**hanksgiving or **S**upplication.

Notes

Bible Study by Chapters

(Form for Pages 194–195)

A. ***Book and Chapter:***

I have ***read*** the chapter carefully, as well as the preceding and following chapter.

Yes ❑   No ❑

B. I would ***title*** this chapter:

C. My simple ***outline*** of this chapter would be as follows:

STUDY

Notes

D. I have ***discovered*** the following in this chapter:

1. The main ***subject*** or ***subjects:***

   ____

   ____

   ____

   ____

2. The ***persons*** revealed:

   ____

   ____

   ____

   ____

3. The ***key verse*** —write it down:

   ____

   ____

   ____

   ____

4. A ***teaching*** about the ***Lord Jesus Christ:***

   ____

   ____

   ____

   ____

5. A ***sin*** I need to confess and forsake:

   ____

   ____

   ____

   ____

Notes

6. A ***command*** I need to obey:

7. A ***promise*** I need to receive:

8. ***Instructions*** I need to follow:

9. A ***prayer*** I should pray:

E. ***List and define*** the key words in this chapter:

STUDY

Notes

F. ***Find*** and ***read*** then ***list*** other scripture references where the main subject of this chapter is discussed in other portions of the Bible.

G., H., I. & J. ***List*** the truths God has revealed to me through this study that I should apply to my life. **Ponder** and **Picture** these truths and then **Pray** these truths back to God as my personal prayer of **A**doration, **C**onfession, **T**hanksgiving or **S**upplication.

STUDY

Notes

II. Bible Study by Paragraphs

A paragraph is a unit of thought in writing, usually containing several sentences. When an author changes his subject of emphasis in his writing, he usually begins a new paragraph. If you wish some help on this, you may look at an American Standard Version of the Bible, the Revised Standard Version of the Bible, or one of the newer translations that prints the Bible text in paragraphs. Studying the Bible by paragraphs like this is often called analytic Bible Study.

A. ***Read*** the paragraph carefully for its main thought or subject.

B. ***Rewrite*** the paragraph in your own words in order to find the relation of the important words and sentences.

C. ***Reread and make*** a simple ***outline*** of the paragraph.

D. With the help of a concordance, ***locate*** in other passages the important words that appear in this paragraph.

E. ***Compare*** this paragraph with other passages of the Bible on the same subject in order not to misunderstand what is meant.

F. ***List the truths*** God has revealed to me through this study that I should apply to my life.

G. **Ponder — *seriously think*** about these truths. What is God saying to me personally?

H. **Picture — *form a mental picture*** of these truths. ***See*** myself in the ***picture*** and ***imagine*** my response.

I. **Pray — *talk to God*** about applying these truths. Pray these truths back to God as my personal prayer of **A**doration, **C**onfession, **T**hanksgiving or **S**upplication.

STUDY

Notes

Bible Study by Paragraphs

(Form for Page 200)

Note: It will be easier for you when studying by paragraphs if you use an American Standard Version, Revised Standard Version or one of the newer translations of the Bible that prints the Bible text in paragraphs.

Book and ***Chapter(s)*** where the paragraph is located:

____

____

A. I have ***read*** the paragraph carefully and discovered the ***main thought*** or ***subject*** to be:

____

____

____

____

____

____

B. In order to find the relation of the important words and sentences, I would ***rewrite*** the paragraph as follows:

____

____

____

____

____

____

____

Notes

C. My simple ***outline*** of this paragraph would be:

D. With the help of a concordance, I have ***located*** the following passages with the same important words that appear in this paragraph. These references and words are:

STUDY

Notes

E. I have ***compared*** this paragraph with other passages of the Bible on the same subject in order not to misunderstand what is meant. These references are:

F., G., H. & I. ***List*** the truths God has revealed to me through this study that I should apply to my life. **Ponder** and **Picture** these truths and then **Pray** these truths back to God as my personal prayer of **A**doration, **C**onfession, **T**hanksgiving or **S**upplication.

STUDY

Notes

III. Bible Study by Verses

In studying the historical passages of the Bible, such as much of the Old Testament or parts of the gospels, each verse may have only one simple meaning. But many verses in both the Old and New Testaments are rich with many great Bible truths that will demand more detailed study.

A. There are many ways that you can study a single Bible verse such as:

1. ***List*** the ***verbs*** and/or ***nouns*** in the verse.
2. ***List*** the ***personalities*** revealed in the verse.
3. ***List*** the ***great ideas*** revealed in the verse.
4. ***Combine*** the various ***ideas*** to grasp the truth being revealed.

B. ***List the truths*** God has revealed to me through this study that I should apply to my life.

C. **Ponder — *seriously think*** about these truths. What is God saying to me personally?

D. **Picture — *form a mental picture*** of these truths. ***See*** myself in the ***picture*** and ***imagine*** my response.

E. **Pray — *talk to God*** about applying these truths. Pray these truths back to God as my personal prayer of **A**doration, **C**onfession, **T**hanksgiving or **S**upplication.

STUDY

Notes

Bible Study by Verses

(Form for Page 204)

Where is the verse ***located:*** ______________________________

I have ***read*** the verse carefully, as well as the preceding and following verses. **Yes** ❑ **No** ❑

A. I have ***discovered*** the following in this verse:

1. The ***verbs:***

____

____

____

____

The ***nouns:***

____

____

____

____

2. The ***personality*** traits of people revealed:

____

____

____

____

3. The ***great ideas*** revealed:

____

____

____

____

Notes

4. To grasp the truth being revealed, I would ***combine*** the various ***ideas*** as follows:

B., C., D. & E. ***List*** the truths God has revealed to me through this study that I should apply to my life. **Ponder** and **Picture** these truths and then **Pray** these truths back to God as my personal prayer of **A**doration, **C**onfession, **T**hanksgiving or **S**upplication.

STUDY

Notes

IV. Bible Study by Books

After you have begun to study the Bible by chapters or paragraphs or verses, you will be ready to study the Bible by books.

A. ***Read*** the book through to get the mood and general emphasis of the book.

B. ***Reread*** the book several times, each time ***asking*** yourself one main question and ***jotting down*** the answers you find as you read. Here are some important questions to ask:

First Reading:
What does the book tell me about the author and his circumstances when he wrote?

Second Reading:
What does the book tell me about the people to whom the book was written and their circumstances, needs or problems? These questions are particularly important when you are reading the Epistles of Paul.

Third Reading:

1. What is the central theme or emphasis of the book?
2. What is the key verse in this book?

Fourth Reading:

1. Remembering the theme of the book, see how it is emphasized and developed in the book.
2. Look for any special problems or applications to this theme.

Notes

Fifth Reading:

1. What are the main divisions of the book?
2. Is there any outline apparent in the logical organization and development of the book?
3. Divide the text into paragraphs.
4. Give a title to each paragraph.

Sixth Reading:

1. Look for other facts and/or information.
2. By now certain words stand out in the book. See how often they recur, and note each time and the surrounding circumstances.

C. ***Outline*** the book.
List any problems, questions, words or ideas that require further study by comparison with other passages in the Bible.

D. ***List the truths*** God has revealed to me through this study that I should apply to my life.

E. **Ponder — *seriously think*** about these truths.
What is God saying to me personally?

F. **Picture — *form a mental picture*** of these truths.
See myself in the ***picture*** and ***imagine*** my response.

G. **Pray — *talk to God*** about applying these truths.
Pray these truths back to God as my personal prayer of **A**doration, **C**onfession, **T**hanksgiving or **S**upplication.

STUDY

Notes

Bible Study by Books

(Form for Pages 207–208)

Book ______________________________

A. I have read the book through to get the mood and the general emphasis of the book.
Yes ❑ No ❑

B. To find the answer to the following questions I have reread the book six more times as suggested.
Yes ❑ No ❑

First Reading:
What does the book tell me about the author and his circumstances?

____

____

____

____

Second Reading:
What does the book tell me about the people to whom the book was written:

1. Their circumstances?

____

____

____

2. Their needs?

____

____

____

STUDY

Notes

3. Their problems?

Third Reading:

1. What is the central theme or emphasis of the book?

2. What is the key verse in this book?

Fourth Reading:

1. How is the theme of the book emphasized or developed?

STUDY

Notes

2. Explain, if you found any special problems related to the theme.

How was the central theme applied?

Fifth Reading:

1. What are the main divisions of the book?

2. Is there an outline apparent in the logical organization and development of the book?
   Yes ❑ No ❑

STUDY

Notes

3. If you were to divide the text into paragraphs, which verses would go in which paragraphs?

Paragraph 1	Ch.____	Verse____	thru Ch.____	Verse____
Paragraph 2	Ch.____	Verse____	thru Ch.____	Verse____
Paragraph 3	Ch.____	Verse____	thru Ch.____	Verse____
Paragraph 4	Ch.____	Verse____	thru Ch.____	Verse____
Paragraph 5	Ch.____	Verse____	thru Ch.____	Verse____
Paragraph 6	Ch.____	Verse____	thru Ch.____	Verse____
Paragraph 7	Ch.____	Verse____	thru Ch.____	Verse____
Paragraph 8	Ch.____	Verse____	thru Ch.____	Verse____
Paragraph 9	Ch.____	Verse____	thru Ch.____	Verse____
Paragraph 10	Ch.____	Verse____	thru Ch.____	Verse____
Paragraph 11	Ch.____	Verse____	thru Ch.____	Verse____
Paragraph 12	Ch.____	Verse____	thru Ch.____	Verse____

4. Give a title to each paragraph:

Paragraph 1 ______________________________

____

Paragraph 2 ______________________________

____

Paragraph 3 ______________________________

____

Paragraph 4 ______________________________

____

Paragraph 5 ______________________________

____

STUDY

Notes

Paragraph 6 ______

Paragraph 7 ______

Paragraph 8 ______

Paragraph 9 ______

Paragraph 10 ______

Paragraph 11 ______

Paragraph 12 ______

STUDY

Sixth Reading:

1. What other facts and/or information stand out?

Notes

2. What are the words that stand out in this book? How often do they recur?

______________________________ _____ times

______________________________ _____ times

______________________________ _____ times

______________________________ _____ times

______________________________ _____ times

______________________________ _____ times

______________________________ _____ times

______________________________ _____ times

______________________________ _____ times

______________________________ _____ times

______________________________ _____ times

______________________________ _____ times

______________________________ _____ times

______________________________ _____ times

______________________________ _____ times

______________________________ _____ times

______________________________ _____ times

______________________________ _____ times

______________________________ _____ times

______________________________ _____ times

______________________________ _____ times

______________________________ _____ times

______________________________ _____ times

STUDY

Notes

C. ***Outline*** the book.

Outside the line to the right of the outline, ***list*** any problems, questions, words or ideas that require further study by comparison with other passages in the Bible.

Write out your ***outline*** below.	***Problems, questions, words*** or ***ideas*** requiring further study.

STUDY

Notes

D., E., F. & G. ***List*** the truths God has revealed to me through this study that I should apply to my life. **Ponder** and **Picture** these truths and then **Pray** these truths back to God as my personal prayer of **A**doration, **C**onfession, **T**hanksgiving or **S**upplication.

STUDY

Notes

V. Bible Study by Words

There are two profitable and helpful ways of studying great words or subjects in the Word of God.

A. ***Word Study by Bible Books***
Read a Bible book and ***count*** the number of times a word is used in this book. ***Decide*** if the word that occurs most frequently gives a clue to the primary emphasis of the book.

B. ***General Word Study***
With the aid of a concordance, ***trace*** the occurrences of a word through the Old Testament and then through the New Testament. By doing this we can become more familiar with the great doctrines and principles that the Bible reveals.

C. ***List the truths*** God has revealed to me through this study that I should apply to my life.

D. **Ponder — *seriously think*** about these truths. What is God saying to me personally?

E. **Picture — *form a mental picture*** of these truths. ***See*** myself in the ***picture*** and ***imagine*** my response.

F. **Pray — *talk to God*** about applying these truths. Pray these truths back to God as my personal prayer of **A**doration, **C**onfession, **T**hanksgiving or **S**upplication.

STUDY

Notes

Bible Study by Words

(Form for Page 217)

Word ______________________________

A. **Word Study by Bible Books:**

1. I have chosen and ***read*** the Book of

   ____

   in search of this word.

   YES ❑ NO ❑

2. By my actual ***count*** the word was used ____ times in this book.

   List the scripture references where you found this word.

   ____________ ____________ ____________

   ____________ ____________ ____________

   ____________ ____________ ____________

   ____________ ____________ ____________

   ____________ ____________ ____________

   ____________ ____________ ____________

   I have read and meditated on each scripture reference where I found this word.

   YES ❑ NO ❑

3. List the other words that appear most frequently in this book.

   ________________ ________________

   ________________ ________________

   ________________ ________________

   ________________ ________________

   ________________ ________________

S T U D Y

Notes

4. ***Decide*** if any of these words give a clue to the primary emphasis of the book.

   Which word? ______________________________

   What is the primary emphasis of the book?

   ____
   ____
   ____
   ____
   ____
   ____
   ____
   ____
   ____
   ____
   ____

STUDY

B. General Word Study:

1. With the aid of a concordance, I have ***traced*** the occurrences of this word through the Old Testament.
   YES ❑ NO ❑

2. With the aid of a concordance, I have ***traced*** the occurrences of this word through the New Testament.
   YES ❑ NO ❑

3. The word was used ___ times in the Old Testament.

4. The word was used ___ times in the New Testament.

Notes

5. List the scripture references where you found this word.

6. I have read and meditated on each scripture reference where I found this word.
YES ❑ NO ❑

STUDY

Notes

C., D., E.& F. ***List*** the truths God has revealed to me through this study that I should apply to my life. **Ponder** and **Picture** these truths and then **Pray** these truths back to God as my personal prayer of **A**doration, **C**onfession, **T**hanksgiving or **S**upplication.

STUDY

Notes

VI. Bible Study by Topics

Closely related to the method of study by words, is the study according to great topics or subjects: Bible prayers, Bible promises, Bible sermons, Bible songs, Bible poems, etc.

Or one might study Bible geography by reading rapidly through and looking for rivers, seas, mountains, etc., highlighted in Scripture. For example, the mountain top experiences in the life of Abraham are a thrilling study.

Another challenging study is to read rapidly through the Gospels and Epistles looking for the commands of the Lord to us. The list of Bible topics is unlimited.

Here are some suggestions for Bible Study by Topics:

A. ***Write*** out a description or definition of the topic.

B. With the help of a concordance, ***list*** the Scripture references where this topic appears in the Bible.

C. Beside each reference you list ***write*** out a key phrase that will help you recall the verse at a glance.

D. From the Scripture references, ***study, combine and write out*** the various ideas on the topic to grasp the truth being revealed.

E. ***List the truths*** God has revealed to me through this study that I should apply to my life.

F. **Ponder — *seriously think*** about these truths. What is God saying to me personally?

G. **Picture — *form a mental picture*** of these truths. ***See*** myself in the ***picture*** and ***imagine*** my response.

H. **Pray — *talk to God*** about applying these truths. Pray these truths back to God as my personal prayer of **A**doration, **C**onfession, **T**hanksgiving or **S**upplication.

STUDY

Notes

Bible Study by Topics

(Form for Page 222)

Topic:____

A. ***Write*** out a description or definition of the topic.

B.& C. With the help of a concordance, ***list*** the scripture references where this topic appears in the Bible. To help you recall the verse at a glance, ***write*** out a key phrase by each reference:

Reference	**Key Phrase**

STUDY

Notes

D. From the Scripture references, ***study, combine and write out*** the various ideas on the topic to grasp the truth being revealed.

STUDY

E., F., G.& H. ***List*** the truths God has revealed to me through this study that I should apply to my life. **Ponder** and **Picture** these truths and then **Pray** these truths back to God as my personal prayer of **A**doration, **C**onfession, **T**hanksgiving or **S**upplication.

Notes

VII. Bible Study through Biography

The Bible is a record of God's revealing Himself to men and through men. The Old Testament as well as the New Testament is rich in such biographical studies. Here are a few:

The life of Noah:	Genesis 5:32–10:32
The life of Abraham:	Genesis 12–25
The life of Joseph:	Genesis 37–50
The life of Deborah:	Judges 4, 5

Here are some suggestions for Bible Study through biography:

A. ***Read*** the Bible book or passages in which this person's life is prominent, e.g., Abraham in Genesis 12–25, plus references to Abraham in Hebrews 11 and Romans 4.

B. ***Trace*** the person with a concordance.

C. ***Note:***

1. Indirect references to this person or his life in other portions of the Scripture.
2. What are some different things you have learned about this person such as important events in their life, character qualities, victories or defeats they experienced, etc.?

D. ***List the truths*** God has revealed to me through this study that I should apply to my life.

E. **Ponder — *seriously think*** about these truths. What is God saying to me personally?

F. **Picture — *form a mental picture*** of these truths. ***See*** myself in the ***picture*** and ***imagine*** my response.

G. **Pray — *talk to God*** about applying these truths. Pray these truths back to God as my personal prayer of **A**doration, **C**onfession, **T**hanksgiving or **S**upplication.

STUDY

Notes

Bible Study through Biography

(Form for Page 225)

Person ____________________

____

A. & B. With the aid of a concordance, ***trace*** and ***read*** the Bible book(s) and passages in which this person's life is prominent. List the scripture references you found:

C. ***Note:*** Indirect reference to this person or his life in other portions of Scripture. List these references.

1.

STUDY

Notes

2. What are some different things you have learned about this person such as important events in his life, character qualities, victories or defeats he experienced, etc.?

D., E., F. & G. ***List*** the truths God has revealed to me through this study that I should apply to my life. **Ponder** and **Picture** these truths and then **Pray** these truths back to God as my personal prayer of **A**doration, **C**onfession, **T**hanksgiving or **S**upplication.

STUDY

Notes

Helpful Bible Study Tools

Recommended Study Bibles

All recommended Study Bibles have:

- Introductions, Overviews/Summaries and Outline of each book.
- Thorough cross reference systems.
- Maps, charts and timelines of kings, prophets, NT and OT chronologies.
- Harmony of the Gospels.
- Dictionary/Concordances.
- Topical Indexes.

Other uniquenesses are listed.

Life Application Study Bible in KJV, NKJV, NIV and NLT.
Publisher: *Tyndale House.*
Today's number one selling study Bible! Thousands of life application notes with application-oriented book introductions.

- Over 10,000 Life Application notes help explain God's Word and challenge readers to apply the truth of Scripture to life.
- Personality profiles highlight over 100 important Bible characters.
- 200 thumbnail maps highlight important Bible places and events.
- 260 charts help explain difficult concepts and relationships.
- Words of Christ in red letter.
- Daily reading plan.

MacArthur Study Bible in NKJV.
Publisher: *Thomas Nelson.*
Featuring the word-for-word accuracy of the NKJV, the MacArthur Study Bible is perfect for serious study. It

STUDY

contains thousands of study notes personally written by Dr. MacArthur and informed by the research of scholars at the Master's Seminary.

- Nearly 25,000 notes.
- 200 page topical index.
- Charts of parables, miracles and prophecies.
- Jewish calendar and feasts.
- Diagrams of Jerusalem.
- 12-page Systematic Theology outline.

Ryrie Study Bible in KJV, NAS and NIV.
Publisher: *Moody Press.*
The *Ryrie Study Bible* has long been a favorite among Dispensationalists. It contains Charles Ryrie's verse-by-verse notations.

- Over 12,000 notes in all.
- 200 in-text maps, charts and diagrams.
- Words of Christ in red letter.
- Synopsis of Bible doctrine—a concise and easy-to-understand outline of the major doctrines found in Scripture.

Thompson Chain Reference in KJV, NKJV, NAS and NIV.
Publisher: *B. B. Kirkbride.*
The unique chain-reference system gives you the "big picture" on 7,000 important topics by linking all the verses pertaining to a certain subject together (more than 10,000 references)—right in the margins for quick referencing.

- Dictionary style pronunciation of difficult words for clarity and accuracy.
- Grammatical and translation notes at the bottom of each page.
- Index of reference chains by topic and chain number.

Notes

- 73-page archaeological supplement with black & white photos.
- Hebrew calendar.
- Words of Christ in red Concordance.
- Character & Prominent Bible Character Studies.

Recommended Resources

Comparative Study Bible
Publisher: *Zondervan Publishing.*
This Bible is a valuable resource for gaining new insights into scriptural truths and the relevancy of God's Word. KJV, NIV, AMPLIFIED and the updated NAS are paralleled inside.

The Complete Word Study Dictionary: New Testament
Publisher: *AMG Publishers,* 1992. Spiros Zodhiates.

Theological Wordbook of the Old Testament
Publisher: *Moody Press,* 1980. Laird Harris, Gleason Archer and Bruce Waltke.

Strong's Exhaustive Concordance of the Bible
Publisher: *Holman Bible Publishers.* James Strong.

STUDY

Bible Translation Summaries

NIV (New International Version; 1978). World's best-selling contemporary translation, smooth reading and highly accurate, uses Modern English. Updated: 1983.

- Balance between word-for-word and thought-for-thought.
- 8th Grade Reading Level (GRL).

NIrV (New International Reader's Version; 1997). Translation designed for children and early readers, uses simple and short words, Modern English.

Notes

- Balance between word translation and meaning, with emphasis on meaning for simplification.
- 3rd GRL.

KJV (King James Version; 1611). Traditionally loved and accepted translation, known for its poetic, dignified presentation of Scripture in 17th Century English.

- Priority to word translation rather than meaning.
- 12th GRL.

NKJV (New King James Version; 1982). Modern language update of the KJV, easier word usage while still using 17th Century sentence structure.

- Priority to word translation rather than meaning.
- 9th GRL.

Living (Living Bible; 1971). Very popular paraphrase of the Bible, purpose of the work was to explain the Bible in simple everyday English.

- Meaning all-important.
- 8th GRL.

NLT (New Living Translation; 1996). Dynamic equivalence translation developed by scholars sought to produce the closest natural equivalent to the message in contemporary English.

- Priority to meaning rather than word translation.
- 6th GRL.

STUDY

Notes

NAS (New American Standard; 1971). Most widely used literal translation for readers who prefer a word-for-word approach. NASB updates the American Standard Version into more current English. Updated: 1995.

- Priority to word translation rather than meaning.
- 11th GRL.

Amplified (Amplified; 1964). Popular translation used to help understand the hidden meaning of the original Greek and Hebrew languages, expanded Bible text with added synonyms, explanatory notes in parentheses, a unique system of punctuation, italics and references. Updated: 1987.

- Priority to word translation plus additional amplification of word meaning.

Source: Zondervan Publishing Bible Translation Chart

STUDY

For free internet access to Bible study resources try:

blueletterbible.org
christianitytoday.com
BibleGateway.com
Gospelcom.net
discipleshiplibrary.com

Please note:
If you are interested in buying books, the following company sometimes sells them at a large discount:

Christian Book Distributors
P. O. Box 7000
Peabody, MA 01961-7000

Phone: 1.800.247.4784
Website: christianbook.com

Memorize

Notes

Passing It On—That's What It's All About

It seems like just yesterday a bunch of us got on our knees in that cold, dark basement in Brunswick, Maine and prayed to commit the time to the Lord. Our goal? To know Christ more deeply and intimately. That was July of 1988. It changed us. A lot of us "grew up in the Lord" that summer. Learning to ponder, picture and pray Scripture made it come alive, and helped me to hide God's Word in my heart. *One on One* gave me the tools to develop a closer walk with Jesus. I have had the privilege of leading others through *One on One* over the years, and to see them grow is truly exciting. And that's what it's all about. Pass it on!

Tom Ackerman, Classic Connections,
Quality Fishing & Hunting Excursions

MEMORIZE

Notes

Scripture Memory Challenge

Have these verses memorized for the following sessions:

1. **Trusting Promises**
   These promises will become anchors for your soul, no matter how rough the water may get in the storms of life.

Session #8	Salvation	John 5:24 John 10:28
Session #9	Deliverance Strength	1 Corinthians 10:13 2 Corinthians 12:9
Session #10	Comfort Needs	1 Peter 5:7 Philippians 4:19
Session #11	Direction Forgiveness	Proverbs 3:5–6 1 John 1:9

2. **Witnessing**

Session #12	Romans 3:23 Romans 6:23 John 3:16
Session #13	John 1:12 Ephesians 2:8–9

3. **Commitment – Yielding – Abiding**

Session #14	Luke 9:23 Romans 6:13 John 15:4

4. **Value of God's Word**

Session #15	2 Timothy 3:16–17 Hebrews 4:12

5. **Encouragement**

Week following Session #15	Isaiah 41:10 Jeremiah 29:11 (LIV) (See Page 188)

In the coming weeks, continue memorizing two verses each week. You will probably choose these verses from what you've read, studied or heard in a sermon or lesson.

MEMORIZE

Notes

Scripture Memory Plan

1. Memorize two new verses each week.
2. **Helps on How to Memorize:**

   a) ***Read the context of the verse in your Bible.*** This helps you understand the verse in its proper setting.

   b) ***Read the verse through several times,*** thoughtfully, aloud or in a whisper. This will help you grasp the verse as a whole.

   c) It is helpful to write the verse out as part of the process of learning. Therefore, ***write the verse out on a verse card.*** Doing this makes a particularly strong impression on the mind. Some people find it helpful to write the verse down several times.

   d) ***Meditate on the verse—*****Ponder** the verse, **Picture** the verse and then **Pray** the verse back to God as your personal prayer of **A**doration, **C**onfession, **T**hanksgiving or **S**upplication.

   e) ***Break the passage into its natural phrases.*** Learn the reference and the first phrase. Then repeat the reference and the first and second phrases. Continue adding phrases until the whole verse is memorized.

   f) ***Review the verse immediately after you have initially memorized it*** by quoting reference, verse, reference 30 times, and then place the day's date on the card.

   g) ***Share the verse with others***—use it or lose it.

   h) ***Review the verse every day for the next two months*** (approximately 60 days) quoting reference, verse, reference each day. This means that your maximum number of verses on any given day will total 16 verses—reviewing 14 past verses and 2 new verses. At the end of two months put the verse back for occasional review and/or future reference.

MEMORIZE

Notes

Excuses & Scriptural Responses

The following are scriptural answers for the excuses men often use for not receiving Jesus as Savior and Lord.

	Excuse	Scriptural Response
1.	I'm not so bad.	Romans 3:10
2.	I'll take my chances.	Hebrews 10:31
3.	I can't understand.	1 Corinthians 2:14
4.	I don't see the need.	John 3:19–20
5.	I'm not good enough yet.	Ephesians 2:8–9
6.	I'm too great a sinner.	Isaiah 1:18
7.	I fear others.	Proverbs 29:25
8.	I couldn't hold out.	1 Peter 1:5
9.	I'll wait till later.	Proverbs 27:1
10.	I want my fun now.	Ecclesiastes 11:9
11.	Too many hypocrites.	Romans 14:12
12.	It doesn't sound reasonable.	Isaiah 55:8–9
13.	I don't believe in Christ.	Romans 3:3
14.	I am an atheist.	Psalm 14:1
15.	What about other religions?	Isaiah 43:11
16.	I don't believe in hell.	Matthew 25:41
17.	Man wrote the Bible.	2 Timothy 3:16
18.	Too much to give up.	Matthew 6:33
19.	______________	______________
20.	______________	______________
21.	______________	______________
22.	______________	______________
23.	______________	______________
24.	______________	______________
25.	______________	______________
26.	______________	______________
27.	______________	______________
28.	______________	______________
29.	______________	______________
30.	______________	______________

MEMORIZE

Notes

Log of Verses Memorized

Date Memorized	Reference	Topic or Key Thought
	John 5:24	Salvation
	John 10:28	Salvation
	1 Cor. 10:13	Deliverance
	2 Cor. 12:9	Strength
	1 Peter 5:7	Comfort
	Phil. 4:19	Needs
	Prov. 3:5–6	Direction
	1 John 1:9	Forgiveness
	Romans 3:23	Witnessing
	Romans 6:23	Witnessing
	John 3:16	Witnessing
	John 1:12	Witnessing
	Eph. 2:8–9	Witnessing
	Luke 9:23	Commitment/Deny Self
	Romans 6:13	Yielding
	John 15:4	Abiding
	2 Tim. 3:16–17	Value of God's Word
	Heb. 4:12	Value of God's Word
	Isa. 41:10	Encouragement
	Jer. 29:11 (LIV)	Encouragement

MEMORIZE

Assignment

ASSIGNMENT

There Was No One There to Help Me

After I accepted Christ at the age of 21, I longed for someone to show me what to do—to disciple me—but no one really knew what to do. They told me to read my Bible. I thought Bible studies were the answer, but none of the popular studies taught me how to have fellowship with God—they taught me about God. *One on One with God* is you and God with no one between. I discovered that God is my everything—Deliverer, Healer, Comforter, Strength, Redeemer and Encourager. I discovered it for myself as I came to Him daily through His Word. He was my teacher. Two years ago God gave me these verses: "*. . .You are to help your brothers until the Lord gives them rest, as He has done for you, and until they too have taken possession of the land that the Lord your God is giving them . . .*" (Joshua 1:14-15). This is my passion —to disciple women—*to help them take possession of the land that God has already given them in Christ Jesus.* So in the last two years I have made many disciples who are now making disciples.

Patty McCargar
Church Secretary

I Found the Missing Link, A Complete Tool

One on One with God has been the missing link for my Christian life, as it influences others. I had nothing to offer those I had led to Christ. All the Bible studies and Christian training I had were all about me. *One on One with God* gave me a complete tool. Jesus Christ gives us the command to go and make disciples, and with *One on One with God,* I can do what He commanded. As a disciple maker, from my home, the Lord has made disciples through me from different denominations, circles of friends and careers, and has also greatly influenced my two preschoolers.

Kristn Punjabi
Homemaker, friend

You Can Have a Fruitful Ministry Anywhere in the World

One on One with God is one of the most effective training tools that we have used. We have more and more students learning to walk with God and becoming competent leaders as a result of this material. I am confident that anyone who learns and lives out the concepts found in *One on One with God* can have a fruitful ministry anywhere in the world. Years ago, *One on One* challenged me to walk with the Lord and helped to make me an effective leader. I highly recommend this training for you to use personally and for an overall strategy for your ministry.

Eddy Pearson
Baptist Collegiate Ministry
University of Arizona

Notes

Assignment . . . . . Prepare for Session 2

1. Explain how to use the "***Follow Up***" sheet (Page 273).
   - Print your ***name.***
   - ***Reporting Date*** is your next meeting date.
   - ***Session #*** is the number of your next meeting.
   - ***Start*** time is just before you pray and ask God to speak to you as you read His Word.
   - ***Stop*** time is when you stop working on your *One on One with God* assignment for the day and have prayed to thank God for the time with Him.

2. Each day read the assigned verses on the ***first month*** "***Daily Bible Reading Challenge***" (Page 49).

3. Write out your answers to the "***Assignment Review Questions***" (Page 242).

4. Ask one person in this class to be your ***prayer partner*** for the next 15 weeks (guys with guys and gals with gals).

Unless one of the codes listed below follows a scripture reference in *One on One with God,* the reference is a quote from the King James Version of the Bible:

AMP — The Amplified Bible
JBP — The New Testament in Modern English (J. B. Phillips)
LIV — The Living Bible (Paraphrased)
MOF — A New Translation of the Bible (James Moffatt)
NAS — The New American Standard Bible
NEB — The New English Bible
NIV — The Holy Bible, New International Version
NKJV — New King James Version
NLT — New Living Translation
RSV — The Revised Standard Version
TCNT — The Twentieth Century New Testament

Notes

Prepare for Session 2
Assignment Review Questions

1. What is Paul trying to communicate in Philippians 3:10 (AMP)?

   That he wants to know God and experance him, and have a strong relationship with Him.

2. What should be the three ***"General Lifetime Goals"*** of a Christian?

   a) To know Him

   b) To Glorify Him

   c) To Be Like Him

3. Why should a Christian be baptized?

   Because it tells us to in the bible and that we should obey every thing the Bible says. Public dispa[illegible] of faith.

4. Have you shared something God is teaching you with someone this week?

   YES ☒ **NO** ❑

ASSIGNMENT

Notes

Assignment . . . . . Prepare for Session 3

- ***Meditate on Philippians 3:10* (AMP)** (Page 9).

1. ***Every day*** fill in the information on the ***"Follow Up"*** sheet (Page 274).

2. *a)* ***Every day*** do the following with the assigned ***first month "Daily Bible Reading Challenge"*** (Page 49):
   (1) ***Read*** the assigned verses (Page 49).
   (2) Make a ***note*** (Page 65—See ***Sample*** on Page 64).
   (3) ***Meditate*** on your note.
      (a) **Ponder** the note.
      (b) **Picture** the note.
      (c) **Pray** the note back to God as your personal prayer of **A**doration, **C**onfession, **T**hanksgiving or **S**upplication.

   b) ***Every day pray*** through the ***"Daily Prayer Reminder"*** (Pages 83–84).

3. ***Review*** the ***"Meditation Challenge"*** (Pages 75–78).

4. ***Review*** and ***Meditate*** on the ***"Prayer Challenge"*** (Pages 81–82).
   a) **Ponder** each thought in the challenge.
   b) **Picture** each thought in the challenge.
   c) **Pray** each thought in the challenge back to God as your personal prayer of **A**doration, **C**onfession, **T**hanksgiving or **S**upplication.

5. ***Write*** out your answers to the ***"Assignment Review Questions"*** (Page 244).

6. ***Watch*** for opportunities to ***share*** what God is teaching you.

ASSIGNMENT

Notes

Prepare for Session 3
Assignment Review Questions

1. List three characteristics of true disciples.

   a) obedient

   b) followers

   c) learners

2. What does it mean to **Ponder?**

   Think about it.
   Seriously think.

3. What does it mean to **Picture?**

   visualize, or a
   mental picture

4. What does it mean to **Pray** back to God as my personal prayer what I have pondered and pictured?

   Talk to God about
   what you have pondered
   and pictured

5. What do the letters in the acrostic **A–C–T–S** stand for?

   A Adoration

   C confession

   T Thanksgiving

   S supplication

6. Have you shared something God is teaching you with someone this week?

   YES ☒ **NO** ❑

ASSIGNMENT

Notes

Assignment . . . . . Prepare for Session 4

- ***Meditate on Philippians 3:10* (AMP)** (Page 9).

1. ***Every day*** fill in the information on the ***"Follow Up"*** sheet (Page 275).

2. *a)* ***Every day*** do the following with the assigned ***first month "Daily Bible Reading Challenge"*** (Page 49):

   (1) ***Read*** the assigned verses (Page 49).

   (2) Make a ***note*** (Pages 65–72).

   (3) ***Meditate*** on your note.

   (a) **Ponder** the note.

   (b) **Picture** the note.

   (c) **Pray** the note back to God as your personal prayer of **A**doration, **C**onfession, **T**hanksgiving or **S**upplication.

   b) ***Every day pray*** through the ***"Daily Prayer Reminder"*** (Pages 83–84).

3. ***Study*** "Allowing Jesus Christ to be the Center and Lord of My Life."

   a) Do some of this study ***each day*** this week during your ***"Quiet Time."*** Read pages 91–97.

   b) ***Fill in*** the blanks.

   c) ***Meditate*** on **(Ponder, Picture** and **Pray):**

   (1) The ***summary*** on page 97.

   (2) The sentences in the study ***where you filled in the blanks.***

   (3) Other ***concepts*** and ***thoughts*** in this study.

4. ***Write*** out your answers to the ***"Assignment Review Questions"*** (Page 246).

5. ***Watch*** for opportunities to ***share*** what God is teaching you.

6. ***Go and make disciples*** (Matthew 28:19 NIV). ***Pray*** that God will lead you to someone whom you can disciple through *One on One with God.*

ASSIGNMENT

Notes

Prepare for Session 4
Assignment Review Questions

1. What are four qualities a true disciple needs to cultivate in his/her life?

   a) Have a heart for the Lord

   b) Be open and teachable

   c) Make oneself available for learning

   d) Willing to sacrifice to learn

2. What does it mean to allow Jesus Christ to be the center and Lord of my life?

   That I no longer desire to run my own life and that I crown Jesus the lord of my life.

3. In this week's study, we read about three reasons why Jesus can and will do a better job of running our lives than we can. What are the three reasons?

   a) He is God!

   b) He is the powerful controller of all things

   c) He is faithful

4. Have you shared something God is teaching you with someone this week?

   YES ☒ **NO** ❑

ASSIGNMENT

Notes

Assignment . . . . . Prepare for Session 5

- ***Meditate on Philippians 3:10* (AMP)** (Page 9).

1. ***Every day*** fill in the information on the ***"Follow Up"*** sheet (Page 276).
2. *a)* ***Every day*** do the following with the assigned ***first month "Daily Bible Reading Challenge"*** (Page 49):
   (1) ***Read*** the assigned verses (Page 49).
   (2) Make a ***note*** (Page 65–72).
   (3) ***Meditate*** on your note:
      (a) **Ponder** the note.
      (b) **Picture** the note.
      (c) **Pray** the note back to God as your personal prayer of **A**doration, **C**onfession, **T**hanksgiving or **S**upplication.

   b) ***Every day pray*** through the ***"Daily Prayer Reminder"*** (Pages 83–84).
3. ***Study*** "Allowing Jesus Christ to be the Center and Lord of My Life."
   a) Do some of this study ***each day*** this week during your ***"Quiet Time."*** Read pages 98–106.
   b) ***Fill in*** the blanks.
   c) ***Meditate*** on **(Ponder, Picture** and **Pray):**
      (1) The ***summary*** on page 106.
      (2) The sentences in the study ***where you filled in the blanks.***
      (3) Other ***concepts*** and ***thoughts*** in this study.
4. ***Read*** and ***meditate*** on **(Ponder, Picture** and **Pray)** the truths in the ***"Daily Commitment Reminder"*** (Pages 31–32).
5. ***Write*** out your answers to the ***"Assignment Review Questions"*** (Page 248).
6. ***Watch*** for opportunities to ***share*** what God is teaching you.
7. ***Go and make disciples*** (Matthew 28:19 NIV). ***Pray*** that God will lead you to someone whom you can disciple through *One on One with God.*

Notes

Prepare for Session 5
Assignment Review Questions

1. What is the formula given to us in Proverbs 3:4–6 (LIV)?
Trust in Christ completely and put him first in everything you do and he will give you direction and success!

2. Name seven things for which we are to trust God daily.
a) Salvation
b) Deliverance
c) Strength
d) comfort
e) needs
f) Direction
g) forgiveness

3. How do we increase or grow the faith God has given us?
Put God first in everything!

4. Have you shared something God is teaching you with someone this week?
YES ❑ **NO** ☒

ASSIGNMENT

Notes

Assignment . . . . . Prepare for Session 6

- ***Meditate on Philippians 3:10* (AMP)** (Page 9).

1. ***Every day*** fill in the information on the **"*Follow Up*"** sheet (Page 277).
2. ***Every day*** do the following:
   a) Complete today's assignment from the **"*Daily Bible Reading Challenge*"** for the ***second month*** **(**Page 50).
      (1) ***Read*** the ***assigned verses*** (Pages 51–62), ***plus*** a chapter each day in ***Proverbs.***
      (2) Make a ***note*** (Pages 65–72).
      (3) ***Meditate*** on your note.
         (a) **Ponder** the note.
         (b) **Picture** the note.
         (c) **Pray** the note back to God as your personal prayer of **A**doration, **C**onfession, **T**hanksgiving or **S**upplication.

   b) ***Pray*** through the **"*Daily Prayer Reminder*"** (Pages 83–84).
   c) ***Read*** through (Page 31) and ***pray*** back to God (Page 32) the **"*Daily Commitment Reminder.*"**
3. ***Study*** "Saturating My Life with God's Word."
   a) Do some of this study ***each day*** this week during your **"*Quiet Time.*"** Read pages 107–119.
   b) ***Fill in*** the blanks.
   c) ***Meditate*** on **(Ponder, Picture** and **Pray):**
      (1) The ***summary*** on page 119.
      (2) The sentences in the study ***where you filled in the blanks.***
      (3) Other ***concepts*** and ***thoughts*** in this study.
4. ***Write*** out your answers to the **"*Assignment Review Questions*"** (Page 250).
5. ***Watch*** for opportunities to ***share*** what God is teaching you.
6. ***Go and make disciples*** (Matthew 28:19 NIV). ***Pray*** that God will lead you to someone whom you can disciple through *One on One with God.*

Notes

Prepare for Session 6
Assignment Review Questions

1. What does it mean to saturate my life with God's Word?

That by consistant daily intake of Gods word the Holy spirit will come into every part of our being

2. What is the value of the diagram related to 2 Timothy 3:16 on page 113?

It shows how Gods word is useful for doctrine, Reproof, correction, and Instruction

3. What must I do to receive the 14 blessings listed on page 118?

For a life Blessed search His word and Obey it!

4. What is the ***"Daily Bible Reading Challenge"*** for the ***Second Month?***

going through the new Testament

5. Have you shared something God is teaching you with someone this week?

YES ☐ **NO** ☒

6. Are you presently leading someone through *One on One with God?*

YES ☐ **NO** ☒

ASSIGNMENT

Notes

Assignment . . . . Prepare for Session 7

- ***Meditate on Philippians 3:10*** **(AMP)** (Page 9).

1. ***Every day*** fill in the information on the ***"Follow Up"*** sheet (Page 278).
2. ***Every day*** do the following:
   a) Complete today's assignment from the ***"Daily Bible Reading Challenge"*** for the ***second month*** (Page 50).
      (1) ***Read*** the ***assigned verses*** (Pages 51–62), ***plus*** a chapter each day in ***Proverbs.***
      (2) Make a ***note*** (Pages 65–72).
      (3) ***Meditate*** on your note.
         (a) **Ponder** the note.
         (b) **Picture** the note.
         (c) **Pray** the note back to God as your personal prayer of **A**doration, **C**onfession, **T**hanksgiving or **S**upplication.

   b) ***Pray*** through the ***"Daily Prayer Reminder"*** (Pages 83–84).
   c) ***Read*** through (Page 31) and ***pray*** back to God (Page 32) the ***"Daily Commitment Reminder."***
3. Use the ***"Sermon or Lesson Notes"*** forms (Pages 21–24) to ***take notes*** this week. ***Meditate*** on your notes—**Ponder** and **Picture** the notes and then **Pray** the notes back to God as your personal prayer of **A**doration, **C**onfession, **T**hanksgiving or **S**upplication.
4. ***Study*** "Saturating My Life with God's Word."
   a) Do some of this study ***each day*** this week during your ***"Quiet Time."*** Read pages 120–128.
   b) ***Fill in*** the blanks.
   c) ***Meditate*** on **(Ponder, Picture** and **Pray):**
      (1) The ***summary*** on page 128.
      (2) The sentences in the study ***where you filled in the blanks.***
      (3) Other ***concepts*** and ***thoughts*** in this study.
5. ***Write*** out your answers to the ***"Assignment Review Questions"*** (Page 252).
6. ***Watch*** for opportunities to ***share*** what God is teaching you.
7. ***Go and make disciples*** (Matthew 28:19 NIV). ***Pray*** that God will lead you to someone whom you can disciple through *One on One with God.*

ASSIGNMENT

Notes

Prepare for Session 7
Assignment Review Questions

1. What are the five methods of saturating my life with God's Word in the "Hand" illustration?

   *a)*________________________________

   *b)*________________________________

   *c)*________________________________

   *d)*________________________________

   *e)*________________________________

2. Explain why the daily, consistent saturating of one's life with God's Word makes a measurable difference in his/her life.

   ____

   ____

   ____

   ____

3. From the summary on page 128, which of the following do you think is the most important?

   A ❑ B ❑ C ❑ D ❑

4. Have you shared something God is teaching you with someone this week?

   YES ❑ NO ❑

5. Are you presently leading someone through *One on One with God?*

   YES ❑ NO ❑

ASSIGNMENT

Notes

Assignment . . . . Prepare for Session 8

- ***Meditate on Philippians 3:10*** (AMP) (Page 9).

1. ***Every day*** fill in the information on the ***"Follow Up"*** sheet (Page 279).
2. ***Every day*** do the following:
   a) Complete today's assignment from the ***"Daily Bible Reading Challenge"*** for the ***second month*** (Page 50).
      (1) ***Read*** the ***assigned verses*** (Pages 51–62), ***plus*** a chapter each day in ***Proverbs.***
      (2) Make a ***note*** (Pages 65–72).
      (3) ***Meditate*** on your note.
         (a) **Ponder** the note.
         (b) **Picture** the note.
         (c) **Pray** the note back to God as your personal prayer of **A**doration, **C**onfession, **T**hanksgiving or **S**upplication.
   b) ***Pray*** through the ***"Daily Prayer Reminder"*** (Pages 83–84).
   c) ***Read*** through (Page 31) and ***pray*** back to God (Page 32) the ***"Daily Commitment Reminder."***.
3. Use the ***"Sermon or Lesson Notes"*** forms (Pages 21–24) to ***take notes*** this week. ***Meditate*** on your notes—**Ponder** and **Picture** the notes and then **Pray** the notes back to God as your personal prayer of **A**doration, **C**onfession, **T**hanksgiving or **S**upplication.
4. ***Study*** "Saturating My Life with Prayer."
   a) Do some of this study ***each day*** this week during your ***"Quiet Time."*** Read pages 129–135.
   b) ***Fill in*** the blanks.
   c) ***Meditate*** on **(Ponder, Picture** and **Pray):**
      (1) The ***summary*** on page 135.
      (2) The sentences in the study ***where you filled in the blanks.***
      (3) Other ***concepts*** and ***thoughts*** in this study.
5. ***Memorize*** and ***meditate*** on **(Ponder, Picture** and **Pray):**
   • John 5:24 • John 10:28
6. ***Write*** out your answers to the ***"Assignment Review Questions"*** (Page 254).
7. ***Watch*** for opportunities to ***share*** what God is teaching you.
8. ***Go and make disciples*** (Matthew 28:19 NIV). ***Pray*** that God will lead you to someone whom you can disciple through *One on One with God.*

Notes

Prepare for Session 8
Assignment Review Questions

1. What does it mean to saturate my life with prayer?

____

____

____

____

2. On page 135, you listed seven reasons why a Christian should saturate his life with prayer. Which one do you think is the most important? Why?

____

____

____

____

3. From the "***Scripture Memory Plan***" we learned that it would be helpful when we are memorizing a verse to review the verse immediately after we have initially memorized it by quoting reference, verse, reference ____ times.

4. Have you shared something God is teaching you with someone this week?

   YES ❑ NO ❑

5. Are you presently leading someone through *One on One with God?*

   YES ❑ NO ❑

ASSIGNMENT

Notes

Assignment . . . . . Prepare for Session 9

- ***Meditate on Philippians 3:10*** (AMP) (Page 9).

1. ***Every day*** fill in the information on the ***"Follow Up"*** sheet (Page 280).
2. ***Every day*** do the following:
   a) Complete today's assignment from the ***"Daily Bible Reading Challenge"*** for the ***second month*** (Page 50).
      (1) ***Read*** the ***assigned verses*** (Pages 51–62), ***plus*** a chapter each day in ***Proverbs.***
      (2) Make a ***note*** (Pages 65–72).
      (3) ***Meditate*** on your note.
         (a) **Ponder** the note.
         (b) **Picture** the note.
         (c) **Pray** the note back to God as your personal prayer of **A**doration, **C**onfession, **T**hanksgiving or **S**upplication.
   b) ***Pray*** through the ***"Daily Prayer Reminder"*** (Pages 83–84).
   c) ***Read*** through (Page 31) and ***pray*** back to God (Page 32) the ***"Daily Commitment Reminder."***
3. Use the ***"Sermon or Lesson Notes"*** forms (Pages 21–24) to ***take notes*** this week. ***Meditate*** on your notes—**Ponder** and **Picture** the notes and then **Pray** the notes back to God as your personal prayer of **A**doration, **C**onfession, **T**hanksgiving or **S**upplication.
4. ***Study*** "Saturating My Life with Prayer."
   a) Do some of this study ***each day*** this week during your ***"Quiet Time."*** Read pages 136–147.
   b) ***Fill in*** the blanks.
   c) ***Meditate*** on **(Ponder, Picture** and **Pray):**
      (1) The ***summary*** on page 147.
      (2) The sentences in the study ***where you filled in the blanks.***
      (3) Other ***concepts*** and ***thoughts*** in this study.
5. ***Memorize*** and ***meditate*** on **(Ponder, Picture** and **Pray):**
   • 1 Corinthians 10:13 • 2 Corinthians 12:9
6. ***Write*** out your answers to the ***"Assignment Review Questions"*** (Page 256).
7. ***Express your love to God three times every hour you are awake this week*** (Psalm 18:1 NIV).
8. ***Watch*** for opportunities to ***share*** what God is teaching you.
9. ***Go and make disciples*** (Matthew 28:19 NIV). ***Pray*** that God will lead you to someone whom you can disciple through *One on One with God.*

Notes

Prepare for Session 9
Assignment Review Questions

1. In prayer I am to be:
   Persistent in **P __ A __ __ N G.**
   Insistent on **G __ __ 'S W __ __ L.**

2. What does it mean to commit yourself to something?

   ____

   ____

   ____

   ____

3. What is the important principle taught in Matthew 6:11?

   ____

   ____

   ____

   ____

4. Have you been consistent in expressing your love to God throughout each day this past week?

   YES ❑ NO ❑

5. Have you shared something God is teaching you with someone this week?

   YES ❑ NO ❑

6. Are you presently leading someone through *One on One with God?*

   YES ❑ NO ❑

ASSIGNMENT

Notes

Assignment . . . . . Prepare for Session 10

- *Meditate on Philippians 3:10* (AMP) (Page 9).

1. *Every day* fill in the information on the *"Follow Up"* sheet (Page 281).
2. *Every day* do the following:
   a) Complete today's assignment from the *"Daily Bible Reading Challenge"* for the *third month* (Page 50).
      (1) *Read* the *assigned verses* (Pages 51–62), *plus* a chapter each day in *Proverbs.*
      (2) Make a *note* (Pages 65–72).
      (3) *Meditate* on your note.
         (a) **Ponder** the note.
         (b) **Picture** the note.
         (c) **Pray** the note back to God as your personal prayer of **A**doration, **C**onfession, **T**hanksgiving or **S**upplication.
   b) *Pray* through the *"Daily Prayer Reminder"* (Pages 83–84).
   c) *Read* through (Page 31) and *pray* back to God (Page 32) the *"Daily Commitment Reminder."*
3. Use the *"Sermon or Lesson Notes"* forms (Pages 21–24) to *take notes* this week. *Meditate* on your notes—**Ponder** and **Picture** the notes and then **Pray** the notes back to God as your personal prayer of **A**doration, **C**onfession, **T**hanksgiving or **S**upplication.
4. *Study* "Saturating My Life with Love."
   a) Do some of this study *each day* this week during your *"Quiet Time."* Read pages 148–154.
   b) *Fill in* the blanks.
   c) *Meditate* on **(Ponder, Picture** and **Pray):**
      (1) The *summary* on page 154.
      (2) The sentences in the study *where you filled in the blanks.*
      (3) Other *concepts* and *thoughts* in this study.
5. *Memorize* and *meditate* on **(Ponder, Picture** and **Pray):**
   - 1 Peter 5:7 • Philippians 4:19
6. *Read* and *meditate on* **(Ponder, Picture** and **Pray)** the truths in *"Caution . . . Caution . . . Caution"* (Pages 25–27).
7. *Write* out your answers to the *"Assignment Review Questions"* (Page 258).
8. *Express your love to God three times every hour you are awake this week* (Psalm 18:1 NIV).
9. *Watch* for opportunities to *share* what God is teaching you.
10. *Go and make disciples* (Matthew 28:19 NIV). *Pray* that God will lead you to someone whom you can disciple through *One on One with God.*

ASSIGNMENT

Notes

Prepare for Session 10
Assignment Review Questions

1. What does it mean to saturate my life with love?

____

____

____

____

2. On page 148, we find that the obedient Christian in action is a loving person. Whom does he/she love?

   a) _______________

   b) _______________

   c) _______________

   d) _______________

3. What is the ***"Daily Bible Reading Challenge"*** for the ***Third Month?***

____

____

____

4. Have you been consistent in expressing your love to God throughout each day this past week?

   YES ❑ NO ❑

5. Have you shared something God is teaching you with someone this week?

   YES ❑ NO ❑

6. Are you presently leading someone through *One on One with God?*

   YES ❑ NO ❑

ASSIGNMENT

Notes

Assignment . . . . . Prepare for Session 11

- ***Meditate on Philippians 3:10*** (AMP) (Page 9).

1. ***Every day*** fill in the information on the ***"Follow Up"*** sheet (Page 282).
2. ***Every day*** do the following:
   a) Complete today's assignment from the ***"Daily Bible Reading Challenge"*** for the ***third month*** (Page 50).
      (1) ***Read*** the ***assigned verses*** (Pages 51–62), ***plus*** a chapter each day in ***Proverbs.***
      (2) Make a ***note*** (Pages 65–72).
      (3) ***Meditate*** on your note.
         (a) **Ponder** the note.
         (b) **Picture** the note.
         (c) **Pray** the note back to God as your personal prayer of **A**doration, **C**onfession, **T**hanksgiving or **S**upplication.
   b) ***Pray*** through the ***"Daily Prayer Reminder"*** (Pages 83–84).
   c) ***Read*** through (Page 31) and ***pray*** back to God (Page 32) the ***"Daily Commitment Reminder."***
3. Use the ***"Sermon or Lesson Notes"*** forms (Pages 21–24) to ***take notes*** this week. ***Meditate*** on your notes—**Ponder** and **Picture** the notes and then **Pray** the notes back to God as your personal prayer of **A**doration, **C**onfession, **T**hanksgiving or **S**upplication.
4. ***Study*** "Saturating My Life with Love."
   a) Do some of this study ***each day*** this week during your ***"Quiet Time."*** Read pages 155–164.
   b) ***Fill in*** the blanks.
   c) ***Meditate*** on **(Ponder, Picture** and **Pray):**
      (1) The ***summary*** on pages 159 and 164.
      (2) The sentences in the study ***where you filled in the blanks.***
      (3) Other ***concepts*** and ***thoughts*** in this study.
5. ***Memorize*** and ***meditate*** on **(Ponder, Picture** and **Pray):**
   • Proverbs 3:5, 6 • 1 John 1:9
6. ***Write*** out your answers to the ***"Assignment Review Questions"*** (Page 260).
7. ***Express your love to God three times every hour you are awake this week*** (Psalm 18:1 NIV).
8. ***Watch*** for opportunities to ***share*** what God is teaching you.
9. ***Go and make disciples*** (Matthew 28:19 NIV). ***Pray*** that God will lead you to someone whom you can disciple through *One on One with God.*

ASSIGNMENT

Notes

Prepare for Session 11
Assignment Review Questions

1. What do you consider to be the most important reason why we should saturate our lives with love for fellow Christians?

___

___

2. What do you consider to be the most important reason why we should saturate our lives with love for the lost?

___

___

3. Can you apply the ***"Principle of Displacement"?*** When?

___

___

4. What does God promise us if we will obey and practice the ***"Principle of Displacement"?***

___

___

5. Have you been consistent in expressing your love to God throughout each day this past week?

   YES ❑ NO ❑

6. Have you shared something God is teaching you with someone this week?

   YES ❑ NO ❑

7. Are you presently leading someone through *One on One with God?*

   YES ❑ NO ❑

ASSIGNMENT

Notes

Assignment . . . . . Prepare for Session 12

- ***Meditate on Philippians 3:10*** (AMP) (Page 9).

1. ***Every day*** fill in the information on the ***"Follow Up"*** sheet (Page 283).
2. ***Every day*** do the following:
   a) Complete today's assignment from the ***"Daily Bible Reading Challenge"*** for the ***third month*** (Page 50).
      (1) ***Read*** the ***assigned verses*** (Pages 51–62), ***plus*** a chapter each day in ***Proverbs.***
      (2) Make a ***note*** (Pages 65–72).
      (3) ***Meditate*** on your note.
         (a) **Ponder** the note.
         (b) **Picture** the note.
         (c) **Pray** the note back to God as your personal prayer of **A**doration, **C**onfession, **T**hanksgiving or **S**upplication.
   b) ***Pray*** through the ***"Daily Prayer Reminder"*** (Pages 83–84).
   c) ***Read*** through (Page 31) and ***pray*** back to God (Page 32) the ***"Daily Commitment Reminder."***
3. Use the ***"Sermon or Lesson Notes"*** forms (Pages 21–24) to ***take notes*** this week. ***Meditate*** on your notes—**Ponder** and **Picture** the notes and then **Pray** the notes back to God as your personal prayer of **A**doration, **C**onfession, **T**hanksgiving or **S**upplication.
4. ***Study*** "Saturating My Life with Love."
   a) Do some of this study ***each day*** this week during your ***"Quiet Time."*** Read pages 165–170.
   b) ***Fill in*** the blanks.
   c) ***Meditate*** on **(Ponder, Picture** and **Pray):**
      (1) The ***summary*** on page 170.
      (2) The sentences in the study ***where you filled in the blanks.***
      (3) Other ***concepts*** and ***thoughts*** in this study.
5. ***Memorize*** and ***meditate*** on **(Ponder, Picture** and **Pray):**
   • Romans 3:23 • Romans 6:23 • John 3:16
6. ***Read*** and ***meditate*** on **(Ponder, Picture** and **Pray)** the truths in ***". . . Blood on Our Hands?"*** (Pages 37–43).
7. ***Write*** out your answers to the ***"Assignment Review Questions"*** (Page 262).
8. ***Express your love to God three times every hour you are awake this week*** (Psalm 18:1 NIV).
9. ***Watch*** for opportunities to ***share*** what God is teaching you.
10. ***Go and make disciples*** (Matthew 28:19 NIV). ***Pray*** that God will lead you to someone whom you can disciple through *One on One with God.*

Notes

Prepare for Session 12
Assignment Review Questions

1. What is the central truth being taught on pages 166–167 (c)?

____

____

____

____

____

2. How can we demonstrate our love for God?

____

____

____

3. Have you been consistent in expressing your love to God throughout each day this past week?

   YES ❑ NO ❑

4. Have you shared something God is teaching you with someone this week?

   YES ❑ NO ❑

5. Have you openly talked about Jesus with someone this week?

   YES ❑ NO ❑

6. Have you invited someone to receive Jesus as his/her personal Lord and Savior this week?

   YES ❑ NO ❑

7. Are you presently leading someone through *One on One with God?*

   YES ❑ NO ❑

ASSIGNMENT

Notes

Assignment . . . . . Prepare for Session 13

- ***Meditate on Philippians 3:10*** (AMP) (Page 9).

1. ***Every day*** fill in the information on the ***"Follow Up"*** sheet (Page 284).
2. ***Every day*** do the following:
   a) Complete today's assignment from the ***"Daily Bible Reading Challenge"*** for the ***third month*** (Page 50).
      (1) ***Read*** the ***assigned verses*** (Pages 51–62), ***plus*** a chapter each day in ***Proverbs.***
      (2) Make a ***note*** (Pages 65–72).
      (3) ***Meditate*** on your note.
         (a) **Ponder** the note.
         (b) **Picture** the note.
         (c) **Pray** the note back to God as your personal prayer of **A**doration, **C**onfession, **T**hanksgiving or **S**upplication.
   b) ***Pray*** through the ***"Daily Prayer Reminder"*** (Pages 83–84).
   c) ***Read*** through (Page 31) and ***pray*** back to God (Page 32) the ***"Daily Commitment Reminder."***
3. Use the ***"Sermon or Lesson Notes"*** forms (Pages 21–24) to ***take notes*** this week. ***Meditate*** on your notes—**Ponder** and **Picture** the notes and then **Pray** the notes back to God as your personal prayer of **A**doration, **C**onfession, **T**hanksgiving or **S**upplication.
4. ***Study*** "Saturating My Life with Love."
   a) Do some of this study ***each day*** this week during your ***"Quiet Time."*** Read pages 171–178.
   b) ***Fill in*** the blanks.
   c) ***Meditate*** on **(Ponder, Picture** and **Pray):**
      (1) The sentences in the study ***where you filled in the blanks.***
      (2) Other ***concepts*** and ***thoughts*** in this study.
5. ***Memorize*** and ***meditate*** on **(Ponder, Picture** and **Pray):**
   • John 1:12 • Ephesians 2:8–9
6. ***Write*** out your answers to the ***"Assignment Review Questions"*** (Page 264).
7. ***Express your love to God three times every hour you are awake this week*** (Psalm 18:1 NIV).
8. ***Watch*** for opportunities to ***share*** what God is teaching you.
9. ***Go and make disciples*** (Matthew 28:19 NIV). ***Pray*** that God will lead you to someone whom you can disciple through *One on One with God.*

Notes

Prepare for Session 13
Assignment Review Questions

1. How does Ephesians 4:32 (NLT) tell us to respond to others?

   *a)*____

   ____

   *b)*____

   ____

   *c)*____

   ____

2. What does Galatians 5:22–25 (LIV) teach us is the key to being a genuine loving person?

   ____

   ____

   ____

3. Have you been consistent in expressing your love to God throughout each day this past week?

   YES ❑ NO ❑

4. Have you shared something God is teaching you with someone this week?

   YES ❑ NO ❑

5. Have you openly talked about Jesus with someone this week?

   YES ❑ NO ❑

6. Have you invited someone to receive Jesus as his/her personal Lord and Savior this week?

   YES ❑ NO ❑

7. Are you presently leading someone through *One on One with God?*

   YES ❑ NO ❑

Notes

Assignment . . . . . Prepare for Session 14

- ***Meditate on Philippians 3:10*** (AMP) (Page 9).

1. ***Every day*** fill in the information on the ***"Follow Up"*** sheet (Page 285).
2. ***Every day*** do the following:
   a) Complete today's assignment from the ***"Daily Bible Reading Challenge"*** for the ***fourth month and thereafter*** (Page 50).
      (1) ***Read*** the ***assigned verses*** (Pages 51–62), ***plus*** a chapter each day in ***Proverbs.***
      (2) Make a ***note*** (Pages 65–72).
      (3) ***Meditate*** on your note.
         (a) **Ponder** the note.
         (b) **Picture** the note.
         (c) **Pray** the note back to God as your personal prayer of **A**doration, **C**onfession, **T**hanksgiving or **S**upplication.
   b) ***Pray*** through the ***"Daily Prayer Reminder"*** (Pages 83–84).
   c) ***Read*** through (Page 31) and ***pray*** back to God (Page 32) the ***"Daily Commitment Reminder."***
3. Use the ***"Sermon or Lesson Notes"*** forms (Pages 21–24) to ***take notes*** this week. ***Meditate*** on your notes—**Ponder** and **Picture** the notes and then **Pray** the notes back to God as your personal prayer of **A**doration, **C**onfession, **T**hanksgiving or **S**upplication.
4. ***Study*** "Saturating My Life with Love."
   a) Do some of this study ***each day*** this week during your ***"Quiet Time."*** Read pages 179–186.
   b) ***Fill in*** the blanks.
   c) ***Meditate*** on **(Ponder, Picture** and **Pray):**
      (1) The ***summary*** on page 186.
      (2) The sentences in the study ***where you filled in the blanks.***
      (3) Other ***concepts*** and ***thoughts*** in this study.
5. ***Memorize*** and ***meditate*** on **(Ponder, Picture** and **Pray):**
   • Luke 9:23 • Romans 6:13 • John 15:4
6. ***Write*** out your answers to the ***"Assignment Review Questions"*** (Page 266).
7. Give yourself the ***test*** on ***"How to Determine the Quality of My Love"*** with one person in mind (Page 30).
8. ***Express your love to God three times every hour you are awake this week*** (Psalm 18:1 NIV).
9. ***Watch*** for opportunities to ***share*** what God is teaching you.
10. ***Go and make disciples*** (Matthew 28:19 NIV). ***Pray*** that God will lead you to someone whom you can disciple through *One on One with God.*

Notes

Prepare for Session 14
Assignment Review Questions

1. A certain spirit is essential to real ***fellowship*** among Christians. The first one listed in this study is a spirit of harmony. What are the other three listed in this study?

   a) Harmony ____________________

   b) ____________________

   c) ____________________

   d) ____________________

2. Paraphrase Colossians 1:28–29 (LIV).

3. How is it possible to love others as much as you love yourself?

4. What is the ***"Daily Bible Reading Challenge"*** for the ***"Fourth Month and Thereafter"?***

5. Have you been consistent in expressing your love to God throughout each day this past week?
   YES ❑ NO ❑

6. Have you shared something God is teaching you with someone this week?
   YES ❑ NO ❑

7. Have you openly talked about Jesus with someone this week?
   YES ❑ NO ❑

8. Have you invited someone to receive Jesus as his/her personal Lord and Savior this week?
   YES ❑ NO ❑

9. Are you presently leading someone through *One on One with God?*
   YES ❑ NO ❑

ASSIGNMENT

Notes

Assignment . . . . . Prepare for Session 15

- ***Meditate on Philippians 3:10*** (AMP) (Page 9).

1. ***Every day*** fill in the information on the ***"Follow Up"*** sheet (Page 286).
2. ***Every day*** do the following:
   a) Complete today's assignment from the ***"Daily Bible Reading Challenge"*** for the ***fourth month and thereafter*** (Page 50).
      (1) ***Read*** the ***assigned verses*** (Pages 51–62), ***plus*** a chapter each day in ***Proverbs.***
      (2) Make a ***note*** (Pages 65–72).
      (3) ***Meditate*** on your note.
         (a) **Ponder** the note.
         (b) **Picture** the note.
         (c) **Pray** the note back to God as your personal prayer of **A**doration, **C**onfession, **T**hanksgiving or **S**upplication.
   b) ***Pray*** through the ***"Daily Prayer Reminder"*** (Pages 83–84).
   c) ***Read*** through (Page 31) and ***pray*** back to God (Page 32) the ***"Daily Commitment Reminder."***
3. Use the ***"Sermon or Lesson Notes"*** forms (Pages 21–24) to ***take notes*** this week. ***Meditate*** on your notes—**Ponder** and **Picture** the notes and then **Pray** the notes back to God as your personal prayer of **A**doration, **C**onfession, **T**hanksgiving or **S**upplication.
4. ***Study*** "Saturating My Life with Love."
   a) Do some of this study ***each day*** this week during your ***"Quiet Time."*** Read pages 187–191.
   b) ***Fill in*** the blanks.
   c) ***Meditate*** on **(Ponder, Picture** and **Pray):**
      (1) The ***summary*** on page 191.
      (2) The sentences in the study ***where you filled in the blanks.***
      (3) Other ***concepts*** and ***thoughts*** in this study.
5. ***Memorize*** and ***meditate*** on **(Ponder, Picture** and **Pray):**
   • 2 Timothy 3:16–17 • Hebrews 4:12
6. ***Write*** out your answers to the ***"Assignment Review Questions"*** (Page 268).
7. ***Express your love to God three times every hour you are awake this week*** (Psalm 18:1 NIV).
8. ***Watch*** for opportunities to ***share*** what God is teaching you.
9. ***Go and make disciples*** (Matthew 28:19 NIV). ***Pray*** that God will lead you to someone whom you can disciple through *One on One with God.*

Notes

Prepare for Session 15
Assignment Review Questions

1. Are you encouraged by Jeremiah 29:11 (LIV)? Why?

____

____

2. Are you encouraged by Psalm 139:1–12, 17–18 (NLT)? Why?

____

____

____

3. What are the four things emphasized on page 191 that will help me develop a strong, healthy, Christ–centered love for myself without becoming prideful?

*a)*_______________

*b)*_______________

*c)*_______________

*d)*_______________

4. Have you been consistent in expressing your love to God throughout each day this past week?

YES ❑ NO ❑

5. Have you shared something God is teaching you with someone this week?

YES ❑ NO ❑

6. Have you openly talked about Jesus with someone this week?

YES ❑ NO ❑

7. Have you invited someone to receive Jesus as his/her personal Lord and Savior this week?

YES ❑ NO ❑

8. Are you presently leading someone through *One on One with God?*

YES ❑ NO ❑

Notes

Assignment . . . . . Until Jesus Comes Again

- ***Meditate on Philippians 3:10 (AMP)*** (Page 9).

1. ***Every day*** do the following:

   a) Complete today's assignment from the ***"Daily Bible Reading Challenge"*** for the ***fourth month and thereafter*** (Page 50).

   (1) ***Read*** the ***assigned verses*** (Pages 51–62), ***plus*** a chapter each day in ***Proverbs.***

   (2) Make a ***note*** (Pages 65–72).

   (3) ***Meditate*** on your note:

   (a) **Ponder** the note.

   (b) **Picture** the note.

   (c) **Pray** the note back to God as your personal prayer of **A**doration, **C**onfession, **T**hanksgiving or **S**upplication.

   b) ***Pray*** through the ***"Daily Prayer Reminder"*** (Pages 83–84).

   c) ***Read*** through (Page 31) and ***pray*** back to God (Page 32) the ***"Daily Commitment Reminder."***

2. Use the ***"Sermon or Lesson Notes"*** forms (Pages 21–24) to ***take notes*** this week. ***Meditate*** on your notes—**Ponder** and **Picture** the notes and then **Pray** the notes back to God as your personal prayer of **A**doration, **C**onfession, **T**hanksgiving or **S**upplication.

3. ***Continue daily Bible Study;*** but now, rather than having printed studies prepared by others, you can ***experience the excitement of discovery on your own.*** Simply choose one of the ***"Methods of Bible Study"*** (Pages 194–227), follow the directions and work on that study as often as possible until it is complete. Then start another study. Be sure to **Ponder, Picture** and **Pray** back to God the truths you discover in each study. You should find the ***"Helpful Bible Study Tools"*** (Pages 228–232) useful in completing these Bible Studies.

Notes

4. ***Memorize*** and ***meditate*** on **(Ponder, Picture** and **Pray):**

   a) During ***this next week:***

   • Isaiah 41:10 • Jeremiah 29:11 (LIV)—see page 188.

   b) During ***the following weeks:***

   Verses that you find that help you or you could use to help others.

5. ***Write*** out your answers to the ***"Assignment Review Questions"*** (Page 271).

6. ***Continue expressing your love, praise and thanks to God throughout each day*** (Psalm 18:1 NIV).

7. ***Watch*** for opportunities to ***share*** what God is teaching you.

8. ***Go and make disciples*** (Matthew 28:19 NIV). ***Pray*** that God will lead you to someone whom you can disciple through *One on One with God.*

9. ***Encourage the group to continue meeting once a month for the next seven months.*** Each person should prepare one Bible Study per month and share it at the monthly meeting. At these meetings agree to be accountable to each other for the other disciplines we have learned (Daily Bible Reading Notes, Sermon or Lesson Notes, Scripture Memory, Prayer and Meditation). Also, agree to be accountable to each other for witnessing to the lost and talking to others about Jesus.

Notes

Assignment Review Questions

1. Paraphrase the four things suggested in the ***"Daily Bible Study Challenge"*** for ***After Session 15,*** that could help me continue to have a meaningful daily Bible Study (Page 192).

   *a)*____

   *b)*____

   *c)*____

   *d)*____

2. What are the seven ***"Methods of Bible Study"*** suggested (Page 193)?

   *a)*____

   *b)*____

   *c)*____

   *d)*____

   *e)*____

   *f)*____

   *g)*____

3. Have you been consistent in expressing your love to God throughout each day this past week?

   YES ❑ NO ❑

4. Have you shared something God is teaching you with someone this week?

   YES ❑ NO ❑

5. Have you openly talked about Jesus with someone this week?

   YES ❑ NO ❑

6. Have you invited someone to receive Jesus as his/her personal Lord and Savior this week?

   YES ❑ NO ❑

7. Are you presently leading someone through *One on One with God?*

   YES ❑ NO ❑

ASSIGNMENT

They Caught The Vision

Our first contact with the Chen/Shih family, former international students from Taiwan, was in 1996. By March 2000, six members of this family were followers of Jesus and approached me about discipling them to help them walk daily with Jesus using *One on One with God.*

Even though my spirit was willing, my flesh was weak—I was recovering from cancer surgery in January. Physically, I didn't feel like I could handle being out another night of the week. But I knew that God was leading me to invest in this family that was hungry for the things of God. Many Thursdays I was so tired I didn't think I could drive to the group meeting. But after about three hours of eating, studying, praying, answering questions (they had a lot of questions), laughing and seeing them grow in Christ before my eyes, I was so excited I couldn't even sleep when I got home late. Their lives were being transformed by the Spirit of God as we met week to week for *One on One with God,* and as they developed the discipline of investing time with Him daily.

By March 2001, there were ten followers of Jesus in this family of former idol worshippers. They are constantly leading others to Christ and discipling them using *One on One with God.* Now I know of fourteen outside the family they have led to Christ. Often they invite unbelievers into their *One on One with God* classes and see them receive Jesus as Lord and Savior.

There is so much to tell about what God is doing through this family. God is using them in a supernatural way. They have a passion to make disciples and multiply. My joy is indescribable as I hear of more fruit each week! I am grateful to God that He led me to invest in this family by helping them learn how to walk with Jesus and giving them principles and a tool to disciple others.

Kirk Goss
Minister of Missions and Collegiate Ministries
Northwest Baptist Church, Oklahoma City, OK

Checked/Initialed by leader

Notes

Follow Up

Name Hannah Guinther

Reporting Date ______

Session # **2**

In your Quiet Time ***each day this week*** note the time you start and the time you stop. This will be the entire time you invest each day to complete your *One on One with God* assignment.

Day	Start Time	Stop Time	Total Time
Monday			
Tuesday	7:45	8:30	45 min
Wednesday	11:30	12:00	30 min
Thursday	6:00	6:15	15 min
Friday			
Saturday	11:10	11:35	25 min
Sunday			0

I am prepared to share or discuss the "Assignment Review Questions":

1. **YES** ☒ **NO** ❑
2. **YES** ☒ **NO** ❑
3. **YES** ☒ **NO** ❑
4. **YES** ☒ **NO** ❑

ASSIGNMENT

Notes

Checked/Initialed by leader

Follow Up

Name ____________________

Reporting Date ____________________

Session # **3**

In your Quiet Time ***each day this week*** note the time you start and the time you stop. This will be the entire time you invest each day to complete your *One on One with God* assignment.			
Day	Start Time	Stop Time	Total Time
Monday	9:00	9:15	15 min
Tuesday	10:40	10:50	10 min
Wednesday	10:05	10:15	10 min
Thursday	12:15	12:25	
Friday			
Saturday			
Sunday	10:15	10:30	13 min

I am prepared to share or discuss the "Assignment Review Questions":

1. **YES** ☒ **NO** ❑
2. **YES** ☒ **NO** ❑
3. **YES** ☒ **NO** ❑
4. **YES** ☒ **NO** ❑
5. **YES** ☒ **NO** ❑
6. **YES** ☒ **NO** ❑

ASSIGNMENT

Checked/Initialed by leader

Notes

Follow Up

Name ______________________________

Reporting Date ______________________________

Session # **4**

In your Quiet Time ***each day this week*** note the time you start and the time you stop. This will be the entire time you invest each day to complete your *One on One with God* assignment.

Day	Start Time	Stop Time	Total Time
Monday			
Tuesday	10:50	11:10	20min
Wednesday	11:40	11:55	15min
Thursday	~~11:45~~		
Friday			
Saturday			
Sunday	11:45	11:55	10min

I am prepared to share or discuss the "Assignment Review Questions":

1. **YES** ☒ **NO** ❑
2. **YES** ☒ **NO** ❑
3. **YES** ☒ **NO** ❑
4. **YES** ☒ **NO** ❑

ASSIGNMENT

Notes

Checked/Initialed by leader

Follow Up

Name ______________________________

Reporting Date ______________________________

Session # **5**

In your Quiet Time ***each day this week*** note the time you start and the time you stop. This will be the entire time you invest each day to complete your *One on One with God* assignment.

Day	Start Time	Stop Time	Total Time
Monday	11:55	12:05	10 mins
Tuesday			
Wednesday			
Thursday			
Friday			
Saturday			
Sunday			

I am prepared to share or discuss the "Assignment Review Questions":

1. **YES** ☒ **NO** ❑
2. **YES** ☒ **NO** ❑
3. **YES** ☒ **NO** ❑
4. **YES** ☒ **NO** ❑

ASSIGNMENT

Checked/Initialed by leader

Notes

Follow Up

Name ______________________________

Reporting Date ______________________________

Session # **6**

In your Quiet Time ***each day this week*** note the time you start and the time you stop. This will be the entire time you invest each day to complete your *One on One with God* assignment.

Day	Start Time	Stop Time	Total Time
Monday			
Tuesday	9:00	9:25	
Wednesday			
Thursday	8:53	9:13	
Friday	3:25	4:25	1 hr
Saturday			
Sunday	10:10	10:50	40 min

I am prepared to share or discuss the "Assignment Review Questions":

1. **YES** ☒ **NO** ❑
2. **YES** ☒ **NO** ❑
3. **YES** ☒ **NO** ❑
4. **YES** ☒ **NO** ❑
5. **YES** ☒ **NO** ❑
6. **YES** ☒ **NO** ❑

ASSIGNMENT

Notes

Checked/Initialed by leader

Follow Up

Name ______________________________

Reporting Date ______________________________

Session # **7**

In your Quiet Time ***each day this week*** note the time you start and the time you stop. This will be the entire time you invest each day to complete your *One on One with God* assignment.			
Day	Start Time	Stop Time	Total Time
Monday			
Tuesday			
Wednesday			
Thursday			
Friday	9:15	10:00	
Saturday			
Sunday			

I am prepared to share or discuss the "Assignment Review Questions":

1. **YES** ❑ **NO** ❑
2. **YES** ❑ **NO** ❑
3. **YES** ❑ **NO** ❑
4. **YES** ❑ **NO** ❑
5. **YES** ❑ **NO** ❑

ASSIGNMENT

Checked/Initialed by leader

Follow Up

Name ______________________________

Reporting Date ______________________________

Session # **8**

In your Quiet Time ***each day this week*** note the time you start and the time you stop. This will be the entire time you invest each day to complete your *One on One with God* assignment.

Day	Start Time	Stop Time	Total Time
Monday			
Tuesday			
Wednesday			
Thursday			
Friday			
Saturday			
Sunday			

I am prepared to share or discuss the "Assignment Review Questions":

1. **YES ❑** **NO ❑**
2. **YES ❑** **NO ❑**
3. **YES ❑** **NO ❑**
4. **YES ❑** **NO ❑**
5. **YES ❑** **NO ❑**

Notes

ASSIGNMENT

Notes

Checked/Initialed by leader

Follow Up

Name ______________________________

Reporting Date ______________________________

Session # **9**

In your Quiet Time ***each day this week*** note the time you start and the time you stop. This will be the entire time you invest each day to complete your *One on One with God* assignment.

Day	Start Time	Stop Time	Total Time
Monday			
Tuesday			
Wednesday			
Thursday			
Friday			
Saturday			
Sunday			

I am prepared to share or discuss the "Assignment Review Questions":

1. **YES ❑** **NO ❑**
2. **YES ❑** **NO ❑**
3. **YES ❑** **NO ❑**
4. **YES ❑** **NO ❑**
5. **YES ❑** **NO ❑**
6. **YES ❑** **NO ❑**

ASSIGNMENT

Checked/Initialed by leader

Notes

Follow Up

Name ____________________

Reporting Date ____________________

Session # **10**

In your Quiet Time ***each day this week*** note the time you start and the time you stop. This will be the entire time you invest each day to complete your *One on One with God* assignment.

Day	Start Time	Stop Time	Total Time
Monday			
Tuesday			
Wednesday			
Thursday			
Friday			
Saturday			
Sunday			

I am prepared to share or discuss the "Assignment Review Questions":

1. **YES ❑** **NO ❑**
2. **YES ❑** **NO ❑**
3. **YES ❑** **NO ❑**
4. **YES ❑** **NO ❑**
5. **YES ❑** **NO ❑**
6. **YES ❑** **NO ❑**

Notes

Checked/Initialed by leader

Follow Up

Name ______________________________

Reporting Date ______________________________

Session # **11**

In your Quiet Time ***each day this week*** note the time you start and the time you stop. This will be the entire time you invest each day to complete your *One on One with God* assignment.

Day	Start Time	Stop Time	Total Time
Monday			
Tuesday			
Wednesday			
Thursday			
Friday			
Saturday			
Sunday			

I am prepared to share or discuss the "Assignment Review Questions":

1. **YES** ❑ **NO** ❑
2. **YES** ❑ **NO** ❑
3. **YES** ❑ **NO** ❑
4. **YES** ❑ **NO** ❑
5. **YES** ❑ **NO** ❑
6. **YES** ❑ **NO** ❑
7. **YES** ❑ **NO** ❑

Checked/Initialed by leader

Follow Up

Name ______________________________

Reporting Date ______________________________

Session # **12**

In your Quiet Time ***each day this week*** note the time you start and the time you stop. This will be the entire time you invest each day to complete your *One on One with God* assignment.

Day	Start Time	Stop Time	Total Time
Monday			
Tuesday			
Wednesday			
Thursday			
Friday			
Saturday			
Sunday			

I am prepared to share or discuss the "Assignment Review Questions":

1. **YES ❑** **NO ❑**
2. **YES ❑** **NO ❑**
3. **YES ❑** **NO ❑**
4. **YES ❑** **NO ❑**
5. **YES ❑** **NO ❑**
6. **YES ❑** **NO ❑**
7. **YES ❑** **NO ❑**

Notes

ASSIGNMENT

Notes

Checked/Initialed by leader

Follow Up

Name ______________________________

Reporting Date ______________________________

Session # **13**

In your Quiet Time ***each day this week*** note the time you start and the time you stop. This will be the entire time you invest each day to complete your *One on One with God* assignment.

Day	Start Time	Stop Time	Total Time
Monday			
Tuesday			
Wednesday			
Thursday			
Friday			
Saturday			
Sunday			

I am prepared to share or discuss the "Assignment Review Questions":

1. **YES ❑** **NO ❑**
2. **YES ❑** **NO ❑**
3. **YES ❑** **NO ❑**
4. **YES ❑** **NO ❑**
5. **YES ❑** **NO ❑**
6. **YES ❑** **NO ❑**
7. **YES ❑** **NO ❑**

ASSIGNMENT

Notes

Checked/Initialed by leader

Follow Up

Name ______________________________

Reporting Date ______________________________

Session # **14**

In your Quiet Time ***each day this week*** note the time you start and the time you stop. This will be the entire time you invest each day to complete your *One on One with God* assignment.			
Day	Start Time	Stop Time	Total Time
Monday			
Tuesday			
Wednesday			
Thursday			
Friday			
Saturday			
Sunday			

I am prepared to share or discuss the "Assignment Review Questions":

1. **YES** ❑ **NO** ❑
2. **YES** ❑ **NO** ❑
3. **YES** ❑ **NO** ❑
4. **YES** ❑ **NO** ❑
5. **YES** ❑ **NO** ❑
6. **YES** ❑ **NO** ❑
7. **YES** ❑ **NO** ❑
8. **YES** ❑ **NO** ❑
9. **YES** ❑ **NO** ❑

Notes

Checked/Initialed by leader

Follow Up

Name ______________________________

Reporting Date ______________________________

Session # **15**

In your Quiet Time ***each day this week*** note the time you start and the time you stop. This will be the entire time you invest each day to complete your *One on One with God* assignment.			
Day	Start Time	Stop Time	Total Time
Monday			
Tuesday			
Wednesday			
Thursday			
Friday			
Saturday			
Sunday			

I am prepared to share or discuss the "Assignment Review Questions":

1. **YES** ❑ **NO** ❑
2. **YES** ❑ **NO** ❑
3. **YES** ❑ **NO** ❑
4. **YES** ❑ **NO** ❑
5. **YES** ❑ **NO** ❑
6. **YES** ❑ **NO** ❑
7. **YES** ❑ **NO** ❑
8. **YES** ❑ **NO** ❑